T0413320

BEATING THE ODDS TOGETHER

50 Years of
Singapore–Israel Ties

BEATING THE
ODDS TOGETHER

50 Years of
Singapore–Israel Ties

Editor

Mattia Tomba
Middle East Institute, National University of Singapore

Published by

World Scientific Publishing Co. Pte. Ltd.

5 Toh Tuck Link, Singapore 596224

USA office: 27 Warren Street, Suite 401-402, Hackensack, NJ 07601

UK office: 57 Shelton Street, Covent Garden, London WC2H 9HE

National Library Board, Singapore Cataloguing in Publication Data
Name(s): Tomba, Mattia, editor.
Title: Beating the odds together : 50 years of Singapore-Israel ties / editor, Mattia Tomba.
Description: Singapore : World Scientific Publishing Co. Pte Ltd, [2020] |
  Includes bibliographical references.
Identifier(s): OCN 1122747159 | ISBN 978-981-121-468-4 (hardback)
Subject(s): LCSH: Singapore--Foreign relations--Israel. | Israel--Foreign relations--Singapore.
Classification: DDC 327.595705694--dc23

British Library Cataloguing-in-Publication Data
A catalogue record for this book is available from the British Library.

Cover image: Singapore's Prime Minister Lee Hsien Loong with Israeli Prime Minister Benjamin Netanyahu during Mr Lee's visit to Israel in 2016, courtesy of the Ministry of Communications and Information.

Back cover image: Israel–Singapore Joint Stamp Issue released in May 2019 to commemorate the 50 years of close bilateral relations, courtesy of Singapore Post and Israel Post.

For any available supplementary material, please visit
https://www.worldscientific.com/worldscibooks/10.1142/11677#t=suppl

Desk Editor: Ong Shi Min Nicole

About the Editor

Mattia Tomba is the founding investor and head of Asia-Pacific at Tradeteq, an electronic trading platform for trade assets. He worked for Qatar's sovereign wealth fund (Qatari Diar), where he managed an equity portfolio and worked on large private equity transactions worldwide. Previously he was part of the Goldman Sachs Group, where he was involved in the investment and portfolio management of large real estate acquisitions in Europe. He began his career with the private wealth management team of Merrill Lynch.

A senior fellow at the Middle East Institute at the National University of Singapore where he focuses on Asia–Middle East relations, Mattia also sits on the advisory council of the Center for Sovereign Wealth and Global Capital at the Fletcher School of Law and Diplomacy at Tufts University. He graduated from the Fletcher School at Tufts University (Boston) with an MA in international affairs and from Bocconi University (Milan)/Sciences Po (Paris) with a BSc in business administration.

Contents

Foreword

The year 2019 marks 50 years of diplomatic relations between Singapore and Israel. However, the ties of friendship between our two countries began in the 1960s, soon after Singapore separated from Malaysia and became an independent state.

The depth of this relationship has rarely been publicised because of political sensitivities, given our neighbours' position towards Israel. This book will fill the lacuna.

Beating the Odds Together commemorates a special relationship that helped lay the foundations of national defence for a fledgling nation. Confidence in Singapore grew in tandem with the establishment of National Service and the building up of the Singapore Armed Forces. Today, we can be open in telling the story of the extraordinary contribution by our Israeli friends to our security when few thought that Singapore could survive on its own.

In 2005, I visited Israel as Senior Minister. Entering Israel via the Allenby Bridge from Jordan, I had a real sense of how exposed Israel was and the harshness of the landscape. I also went up to the Golan Heights. This visit gave me a deeper understanding of the meaning of vulnerability and how resilient and determined the Israelis are to survive as a country. As a similarly vulnerable small state, Singapore must be courageous in ideas, globally competitive and always prepared to tough it out.

Our relationship with Israel has grown stronger. It has gone beyond defence ties. We have a healthy trade relationship. We learn how Israel is adapting to changing demographics, new economic circumstances and rapid technological changes. Israel has a world-class research and development ecosystem and a vibrant start-up scene. Singapore can learn from Israel and collaborate with it in these and other new areas.

Being friends with Israel has not been without controversy. In 1986, the Singapore Government's decision to invite then-President Chaim Herzog was met with anger and criticism from our immediate neighbours. Diplomatic protests were lodged and envoys recalled. In 2017, reactions were a little more muted when Israeli Prime Minister Benjamin Netanyahu made a one-day visit to Singapore. For our part, Singapore has contributed to building a harmonious ASEAN community based on mutual respect.

I look forward to more years of close ties between Singapore and Israel.

Goh Chok Tong
Emeritus Senior Minister
Singapore
December 2019

Goh Chok Tong was Prime Minister of Singapore from 1990 to 2004. He subsequently served as Senior Minister until 2011.

Preface

·

When we reflect on the 50 years of bilateral relations between Israel and Singapore, it is hard to believe that back in the 1960s, nobody in Israel, or in Singapore for that matter, could have remotely envisioned how far those relations could progress.

The Israel of the 1960s was a very different country from what it is today; the same applies to Singapore.

What started out as a necessity for Singapore and an eagerness on the part of Israel to help another country cast off the shackles of colonialism created an alliance beyond anyone's imagination.

At the beginning of this long journey, it was not easy to find common ground between our two countries, our societies and economies. However, destiny and friendship moulded a strong partnership that has lasted 50 years.

In this book, you will find testimonies of some of the people who were the architects of this special relationship between the two states. I feel that the citizens of our countries owe them and many others a debt of gratitude.

The foundations of our bilateral ties are strong, and they will continue to be so for many years to come. We will strive to work together to find unique solutions to mutual challenges as well as to handle common global challenges.

I would like to wish the citizens of Israel and Singapore alike many years of prosperity and continued achievements.

Sagi Karni
Ambassador of Israel to Singapore
December 2019

Sagi Karni assumed the role of Ambassador of Israel to Singapore in August 2019.

Introduction

Mattia Tomba

In 1969, Singapore established diplomatic relations with Israel. In the early years, Singapore wanted its ties with the Jewish state to be kept very discreet in order to maintain good relations with the local Muslim community and the neighbouring Muslim-dominant countries. Though relations between Singapore and Israel started at the security level, eventually they expanded to many other fields, including business, academia, research, culture, technology and education.

In 2019, Singapore and Israel marked the 50th anniversary of their bilateral ties, and we decided to publish this book to celebrate the 50 years of this mutually beneficial relationship between the two countries.

This volume brings together 13 chapters by Singaporeans and Israelis who have made or are making important contributions to the relations between both countries in different fields, and explains the similarities and differences between the two countries. Hailing from different backgrounds and with different experiences, our contributors are former and current diplomats, former ministers, businessmen, rabbis, architects and professors.

Bilahari Kausikan explains the similarities and differences between Israel and Singapore, and how two countries that had to learn to survive in difficult geopolitical environments eventually became close. He also tells us how their identities developed and the challenges they face today.

Winston Choo recounts how this unlikely friendship between two countries from disparate regions has since developed into one founded on mutual understanding and respect, shared values and a forward-thinking outlook. Even as Singapore maintains an important partnership with Israel, the Republic has also developed robust ties with the Palestinian National Authority, founded on technical co-operation to enhance its capacity-building efforts.

Simona Halperin examines the history of Israel–Singapore bilateral ties, showing how they expanded from the area of security to avenues in business, healthcare, academia, education, culture, and research and development.

George Yeo recalls his many visits to Israel and how the working relationships transformed into friendship. He remembers how Ben-Gurion was the only one who responded positively to Lee Kuan Yew's call for help to build up Singapore's defence forces after Nehru and Nasser had both declined. He also recognises that while there are some similarities between Israel's circumstances and Singapore's, the politics of Southeast Asia are, happily, much more benign than the politics in the Middle East.

Peter Ho explains how the defence ties started and were established during the early years. He expresses gratitude that Israel was a friend in need when Singapore's need was greatest. The first Israelis who came to the Republic were called "the Mexicans" to keep the relations between the two countries a secret. The Israeli advisors played a key role in the early years of the Singapore Army, helping the Republic to establish its National Service system, its training system and its military organisation.

Rabbi Jean Pierre Fettmann expounds on the Jewish principle of *tikkun olam*, which is literally translated as "repairing the world", and how it promotes interfaith activities. In Singapore, with the moral and ethical frameworks of *tikkun olam* and interfaith relations provided by their Jewish faith, Jews have helped to play a crucial role in helping the Republic build a society based on peace, harmony and unity.

Victor Sassoon traces the history of Jews in Singapore and their contributions to nation building, starting with the first Jews who arrived as early as 1819, soon after the first British settlement. The Jewish population subsequently expanded in the early part of the 19th century following historic events such as the opening of the Suez Canal. Today Jews in Singapore are from all over the world — from Israel, Europe, the Americas and Asia.

Edmund Lim digs into the history of Jewish synagogues in Singapore that is closely intertwined with the history of the Jewish community. He follows the development of national monuments Maghain Aboth Synagogue and Chesed-El Synagogue from the first synagogue located in a nondescript shophouse near Boat Quay.

Moshe Safdie talks about his association with the Republic, which goes back as far as 1973. He recounts his increasing respect and attachment for a nation that has led the world in embracing a policy of affirmative intervention of individual developments towards achieving a more cohesive and workable city. Among his notable projects in Singapore are: Marina Bay Sands, The Ardmore, The Edge on Cairnhill, Orchard Boulevard and Jewel at Changi Airport.

Raanan Boral revisits the three short, but gloriously free years that he spent as a young child in post-independence Singapore in the 1960s. Nothing, he says, could compare with that experience.

Robyn Klingler-Vidra looks at similarities and differences between Singaporean and Israeli venture capital policies. In particular, she explains how the Republic learnt how to utilise government action to build up a successful venture capital policy from the Start-up Nation.

Mark Shmulevich dissects the unique approaches that Israel and Singapore took in commercialising technological research into real-world innovation. Learning from such approaches can help turn more research projects into technologies and businesses.

Joel Bar-El and Dror Feldheim share with us the founding of Trax and how the first Israeli–Singaporean unicorn could not have been possible without tapping into the best of both countries.

Mattia Tomba
Editor
Middle East Institute
National University of Singapore

Singapore: Israel in Southeast Asia?

Bilahari Kausikan

In the 1960s and 1970s, and up to the 1980s, our neighbours never tired of referring to Singapore as "the Israel of Southeast Asia". It was not meant to be a compliment.

The comparison was intended to remind us of Singapore's essential "otherness" and to question our legitimacy. It was a warning about the vulnerability of an ethnic Chinese majority state in a Malay–Muslim region. The clear implication was that we should subordinate ourselves to their interests as did — and still do — their own Chinese minorities.

When President Chaim Herzog of Israel visited Singapore in 1986, our neighbours reacted with outrage, as if it was not our right to invite anyone we pleased to visit our sovereign territory. In 2017, the far more controversial Prime Minister Benjamin Netanyahu visited Singapore. There was nary a peep from Malaysia or Indonesia.

Our neighbours once saw the United States as an interloper in Southeast Asia. Our close ties with the US and our public support for the vital role that it plays in regional stability was regarded as eccentric, if not downright provocative. Equating Singapore with Israel was perhaps also intended as a reminder that our close relations with America may not save us.

On 9 August 1991, our National Day, Malaysia and Indonesia held a joint military exercise in Johor, very close to our borders. Mr Goh Chok Tong had just replaced Mr Lee Kuan Yew as Prime Minister, and the joint exercise was clearly intended to test the mettle of our new leadership. Just in case we were too obtuse to get the message, the exercise was codenamed *Pukul Habis* —"total wipe out" in Malay.

We do not depend on the US to come to our rescue, other than to sell us the means to defend ourselves. In response to *Pukul Habis*, we mobilised our Singapore Armed Forces (SAF) reserves. New weapons and live ammunition were issued. Armour and artillery were deployed to assembly areas. National Day passed without incident. As far as I am aware, no similar joint exercise has since been held.

In 1990, after the US withdrew from the Philippines, we signed a Memorandum of Understanding (MOU) with the US that allowed the Americans to use some of our facilities. Our neighbours reacted as if we were conspiring with the US to sell their firstborn into slavery. No controversy greeted the renewal of the MOU in 2005. And when we renewed it for a third time in September 2019, it was hardly noticed.

Clearly, something has changed. Our neighbours no longer brandish the comparison with Israel against us, or at least if they do, it is done so discreetly as to have escaped my notice.

Equating Singapore with Israel as a warning is no longer credible. After winning four wars against numerically superior Arab forces, Israel is not going to be pushed into the sea. It is a successful country, here to stay as a legitimate part of the Middle East. The Omani Foreign Minister publicly said so in 2018 to an audience that included several of his counterparts and senior officials from Arab countries. No one present on that occasion demurred.

Common concern over Iran has led several Arab countries to develop their own barely concealed ties with Israel. So has Indonesia, for different reasons. Malaysian Prime Minister Dr Mahathir Mohamed's offensive comments about Israel and Jews come across as embarrassingly and distastefully out of touch. An assertive China has driven home the importance of the American presence to our neighbours.

But have attitudes really changed in any fundamental way? I don't think so. A successful Singapore based on the principle of multiracial meritocracy is an implicit criticism of neighbouring systems based on the diametrically different principle of racial and religious hierarchy. This holds our neighbours back from realising their full potential. Our very existence as a more successful country is a continual reproach that could easily turn their own peoples against their governments.

Unless they change their systems — which is well-nigh impossible — our neighbours will always need an "other" to blame for their own shortcomings. The steady Arabisation of Southeast Asian Islam may over time create common ground that overwhelms the competing Indonesian and Malaysian nationalisms that have so far constrained their ability to forge strategic co-operation against Singapore. We must always keep our powder dry.

When former Indonesian President BJ Habibie dubbed Singapore "a little red dot" in a sea of green, he was trying to evoke the same warnings as comparing Singapore with Israel. It did not work. Singaporeans turned the intended insult into a badge of honour and pride. We were able to do so because we are now strong, for which we have much to thank Israel.

Israel helped us build the Singapore Armed Forces (SAF) into a credible deterrent force — the most technologically advanced and capable in Southeast Asia — at a time when no other country would. No other country was then willing to help, for the simple reason that they thought we would not survive. It was then not unreasonable to think so. For Israel to have helped us was an act of faith, not logic. I am still not sure why Israel did so. Perhaps it was empathy for another small country in a precarious geopolitical situation. Whatever the reason, it was an act for which we should be profoundly grateful, and which young Singaporeans of all ethnicities should better understand.

Lee Kuan Yew once told an Israeli general who had helped start the SAF that Singapore had learnt two things from Israel: how to be strong, and how not to use our strength. What he meant was that it was necessary to get along with neighbours and that no country, however strong, can live in a perpetual state of confrontation with them.

Strong deterrence is a necessary condition for good relations with neighbours. But military deterrence is in itself an insufficient condition. Strong deterrence keeps neighbours honest and creates the opportunity to build co-operative ties. The opportunity has to be used, and we have used it to a far greater extent than Israel. Co-operation between Singapore and all our neighbours, however difficult, and whether through ASEAN or bilaterally, is an imperative of our foreign policy.

Of course, we do not face the same level of threat that Israel confronts on a daily basis. Iranian leaders threaten to "wipe Israel off the map". Within living memory, Arab leaders have made similar threats. None of our neighbours is trying to acquire nuclear weapons. Our neighbours want to subordinate us, not destroy us. They may under-perform economically, but they do well enough. None of Israel's neighbours are economically successful. Some are very rich, but that is not the same thing.

I think most Israelis know that the present attitude of Arab governments towards Israel could change very rapidly if it suits their interests. They may hope otherwise, but hope is just that. No Arab government is today as invested in the Palestinian issue as in the past. But Israel's neighbours will always need an issue to blame for their own failures of governance and to distract their restive populations. If not Palestine, they will have to invent something else. Which is not to say that the Palestine issue could not be better managed by all parties concerned.

Israel and Singapore are improbable countries: We should not exist. Yet here we both are and here we both intend to stay, working together as we often do, pursuing our own interests when we must. The primary threats faced by Israel and Singapore are today internal, not external. If we fail, it will be our own fault. At root, the essential issues for both of us arise from questions of identity.

Israel and Singapore are outliers in our respective regions. *And we both must always be outliers if we are to continue to survive and prosper.* If Israel becomes just another Middle Eastern country, or Singapore becomes just another Southeast Asian country, we cannot survive, let alone prosper. For both Israel and Singapore, albeit for very different reasons, the complications of identity and the risk of becoming just like our neighbours cannot be ignored. They are real.

Singapore and Israel are small countries. Small countries have no intrinsic relevance in the international system. For small countries, relevance is an artefact to be created and maintained by human endeavour.

The fundamental basis of creating and maintaining relevance is to be exceptional. This does not make us dearly loved by our neighbours, but it cannot be helped. It is the existential condition of being Israeli or Singaporean. Nobody ever promised that it was going to be easy to be Israeli or Singaporean. But at this point, the similarities between our countries begin to diverge.

After the pogroms of the 19th century and the Holocaust of the 20th century, the basic raison d'être of the Zionist movement, and hence of Israel after 14 May 1948, was the survival of the Jews — physical survival. Millennia before a Jewish homeland was re-established, there was a Jewish nation. After 1948, an inconvenient but unavoidable question arose and over time intruded ever more insistently: Who is an Israeli?

Twenty-one per cent of Israel's population is Arab. The growth rates of Israel's Arab and Jewish populations are equalising. In 2013, the former grew at slightly over 2 per cent and the latter at 1.7 per cent. But the rise in Jewish population growth is primarily due to Orthodox Jews, particularly the ultra-Orthodox. Relations between secular and ultra-Orthodox Jews are fraught with tensions which ultimately relate to the identity of Israel. All Jews are nevertheless forever bound together in a symbiotic dialectic — can there be an idea of the secular apart from the idea of Orthodoxy? — in a way which Arab Israelis and Jewish Israelis are not bound together, or at least, hopefully, not yet.

Still, why should there be an Israel if it is not to be the homeland of the Jews? Why should the Jews not have a homeland? Can there be Jews without Judaism in all its bewildering (to a Gentile) graduations and variations? What is the status of Arabs in a Jewish state? Is there a contradiction between the idea of Israel as a democracy and the idea of Israel as a Jewish state? Palestine is an issue with no perfect solutions. But some sort of answers to these questions — or at least workable compromises — cannot be forever postponed without Israel risking becoming just like its neighbours.

In Israel, questions of identity arise because Israel is an "Old New Land", to quote the title of a novel by Theodor Herzl, the founder of political Zionism. Singapore's questions of identity arise because we are a very new, new land — 54 years is but an instant in the long sweep of history.

Singapore and Israel are countries of immigrants. But for Jews, becoming Israeli is fundamentally a question of "return", of making *Aliyah*. The ancestors of Singaporeans were sojourners. None of our forefathers came to Singapore with the idea of "becoming Singaporean". The concept did not then exist. And even when the twists and turns of history made returning to ancestral homelands impractical or undesirable, few, if any, conceived of a Singaporean identity apart from a broader "Malayan" identity.

Speaking in the Singapore Legislative Assembly on 5 March 1957, Mr Lee Kuan Yew said: "In the context of the second half of 20th century Southeast Asia, island nations are a political joke." Lee's statement underscored his conviction that merger with Malaya was the only practical way forward.

Our first-generation leaders were emotionally attached to the idea of Malaya, and did not believe that Singapore could survive detached from our traditional hinterland. When it became inescapably evident that their ideal of a "Malaysian Malaysia" in which all ethnicities would be equal was absolutely unacceptable to Malay leaders in Malaysia, and that Separation was the only alternative to bloodshed, some were reluctant to accept the new reality. Lee wept during the televised press conference announcing Singapore's independence. He may have thought that all was lost.

But it was not. Having risked independent Singapore becoming a "political joke" for the sake of an ideal, we had to make the ideal work. And we did, with the government and people pulling together under very dangerous conditions. It was sometimes a close-run thing. Fortunately, we did not make irretrievable errors. But there was certainly plenty of trial.

The Singaporean identity is today a reality. Few, if any, Singaporeans would be willing to contemplate re-merger with Malaysia. We are clearly better off out than in. But the Singaporean identity is nevertheless new and perhaps still shallow, or at least malleable in a way that Jewish identity, despite all its internal tensions, is not.

A casual observer of Israel might be forgiven for concluding that Israelis live in a continual state of contention. This is a superficial view. Israelis fight very fiercely over the meaning of being Jewish or being Israeli. But few doubt that they are in some sense Jewish, or that Israel's essential raison d'être is to be the homeland of the Jews. Outsiders unwary enough to be tempted to intervene in these internal Israeli quarrels will soon find that they will stop quarrelling and beat you up so as to be left to fight in peace.

The meaning of being Singaporean does not have this underlying bedrock of consensus hammered into Jews of all persuasions by millennia of exile and persecution. In Southeast Asia, all other societies, without exception, organise themselves vertically: on the basis of formal or informal ethnic or religious hierarchy. Our unique horizontal organising principle of multiracial meritocracy is a strength that Israel, for all its other strengths, does not enjoy, and because of its historical founding premises, perhaps cannot enjoy.

But Singapore's exceptionalism is not a self-sustaining condition. The challenge for Singapore is to be part of our region without being trapped within it or becoming just like it. We live in an age where hierarchical identities of various kinds are being asserted, sometimes as a deliberate instrument of state policy, sometimes through the operation of broader social, cultural and economic trends, or through some combination of both.

It would be foolish to believe that we are somehow immune to, or can be completely insulated from, these centrifugal forces.

Our exceptionalism must therefore be continually defended by the exercise of state power, if necessary, prophylactically and without hesitation, indeed ruthlessly. That in turn requires maintaining the neutrality of the state and government. This is not to be taken for granted and will probably become more difficult. In democracies, some will always be tempted to use ethnicity or religion for partisan advantage. Early symptoms have already appeared. As our politics grow more complicated, the temptation will increase. If opposition politicians have so far resisted the temptation, is it because of fear, or conviction?

Nobody harbours the idea of trying to drive Singaporeans into the sea or wipe us off the map. None of our neighbours has the capability to do so. There is no "anti-Singaporeanism" in Southeast Asia in the same sense as there still is, unfortunately, antisemitism in the West and Middle East. But if the social compact of multiracial meritocracy on which Singapore is based is broken, it will be extremely difficult, if not impossible, to put it together again. We will then risk becoming just another Southeast Asian country.

I am not unduly pessimistic about the future of either Israel or Singapore. Small countries, however dire their circumstances may appear, are never entirely without agency, and can use it. That is why we exist. We forget that only at our own peril.

If this truth is more evident to Israelis than most Singaporeans, it is because the challenges and tensions that Israel has always had to confront have always had a far greater and compelling immediacy than those Singapore must now face. We have perhaps been too successful too quickly, and thus grown somewhat complacent, sometimes reluctant to act decisively. But our challenges, while seemingly less immediately dangerous, are no less real.

When Israel makes mistakes, they are usually mistakes of action without adequate long-term planning. But that willingness to take risks — Israel cannot afford the luxury of not exercising agency — is the ultimate source of Israeli creativeness, spirit, and genius for improvisation. Singapore excels at long-term planning. But I fear that Singapore's mistakes will be those of excessive caution. Not everything can be planned; not all plans will unfold as anticipated. Small countries have narrow margins for error. But sometimes, the biggest risk is trying to avoid all risks.

Perhaps Israel should become a little more like Singapore, and Singapore a tad more like Israel — just a tad.

Bilahari Kausikan is Chairman of the Middle East Institute. He was formerly Permanent Secretary of Singapore's Ministry of Foreign Affairs.

A Special Relationship that Continues to Grow

Winston Choo

Singapore and Israel share a special relationship, initially born of necessity. As a newly-independent state with limited resources other than our people and sheer grit to rely on, Singapore needed Israel's help to build up our armed forces. As it turned out, Israel also sought a friend in the region. This unlikely friendship of two countries from disparate regions has since developed into one founded on mutual understanding and respect, shared values and a forward-thinking outlook. While our ties are strong, this special relationship has its trials, too. But reinforcing our bonds is the shared determination to thrive and build a brighter future for our peoples amid challenging circumstances. Ultimately, the mutual trust and respect that undergirds our relationship cannot be taken for granted.

When Singapore stumbled into independence and our security and survival were in doubt, Israel provided ready assistance for the establishment of our armed forces. This was despite other states turning down our requests for help. The Israelis readily drew up a plan to build up a credible Singapore Armed Forces within a relatively short time frame. This plan was anchored by a conscription system like Israel's, mobilising citizens to serve in the armed forces.

However, the Israeli military advisers' presence in Singapore presented us with an awkward political quandary. The Israeli–Palestinian conflict was, and still is, an emotive and salient issue among Southeast Asian Muslims.

But Singapore was vulnerable, with few options. Therefore, we had to keep our defence co-operation low-profile to avoid riling up sensitivities. We even referred to the Israeli military advisers as the "Mexicans" to cover up their true identities. The subterfuge did not hinder the development of substantive co-operation. We remain grateful for the Israelis' helping hand in our time of need.

Singapore's continued engagement of Israel is far from problem-free. Then-Israeli President Chaim Herzog's visit to Singapore as part of his Asia-Pacific tour in 1986 was met with intense unhappiness from our Muslim-majority neighbouring countries, which called for Singapore to be more considerate of Muslim sympathies for the Palestinian cause. It was a fraught period for Singapore's relations with our closest neighbours, but we stood firm and weathered the storm. That episode reminded us of the value of mutual empathy and respect, the fragility of peace in a multicultural region, and the importance of maintaining a principled position on international issues.

Over the years, the bilateral friendship has been augmented by mutual respect and trust. We continue to nurture our relations with Israel while maintaining a principled position and respecting the differing stances and sentiments towards the Middle East peace process. At international fora, particularly at the United Nations, Singapore has maintained our longstanding and consistent support for a negotiated two-state solution with Israel and Palestine living side-by-side in peace and security. The Israeli–Palestinian conflict is a complex issue with a long history. Singapore is not alone in harbouring the hope that both sides will arrive at an enduring and just solution, which will be good for the Middle East and the rest of the world. Meanwhile, as we keep up our important partnership with Israel, we have also developed robust ties with the Palestinian National Authority, founded on technical co-operation to enhance their capacity-building efforts.

Although Singapore and Israel differ in terms of politics and governance, a shared focus on self-sufficiency and progress has been a driving factor in the expansion and diversification of our bilateral ties. Our ties had been driven by defence co-operation, but bilateral co-operation has since expanded and diversified to other sectors, such as technology, research and development (R&D) and education. These are areas in which the exchange of knowledge and expertise would reap significant mutual benefit. After all, innovation and enterprise are important pillars of both countries' economies and allow Singapore and Israel to punch above their weights. The Israelis' risk-taking and inventive spirit has facilitated the development of dynamic domestic industries in R&D and entrepreneurship, which Singapore could learn from. The Singapore–Israel Industrial Research & Development Foundation (SIIRD), incorporated in 1997, is a flagship economic bilateral initiative that facilitates R&D collaboration between Israeli and Singaporean entities. Our National Research Foundation also enjoys robust links with Israeli tertiary institutions in the areas of cybersecurity, computer science and life sciences.

The ties between our peoples also have grown over the years. Despite the geographical distance between Singapore and Israel, our respective societies have a common aspiration towards creating a sense of shared nationhood among diverse communities. The dynamism and experience of the thriving Jewish diaspora and Israelis continue to contribute to the vibrancy of Singapore's society. In fact, the contributions of the Jewish diaspora to Singapore pre-date our independence. Our first Chief Minister, David Marshall, was born in Singapore to Jewish migrants from Baghdad. Mr Moshe Safdie is a renowned Israeli architect behind two Singaporean icons — Marina Bay Sands and Jewel Changi Airport. There is greater awareness of Israeli culture in Singapore, spread by the likes of the annual Israel Film Festival, distinguished performances by the Israel Philharmonic Orchestra, and the availability of Israeli food. A growing number of Singaporeans are also visiting Israel for more varied purposes, including work, studies and leisure. In addition, religious pilgrims make up a significant proportion of Singaporean travellers to Israel.

Our special relationship continues to grow from strength to strength. The ebb and flow of challenges and opportunities over the past 50 years has led to an increasing number of high-level exchanges and ministerial visits. These culminated in the bilateral milestones of the reciprocal visits by

Prime Minister Lee Hsien Loong to Israel in 2016 and Israeli Prime Minister Benjamin Netanyahu to Singapore in 2017. Looking towards the next 50 years, our intertwined geopolitical realities in the Middle East and Asia lend weight to enhancing bilateral co-operation to address more complex global challenges. These modern transboundary challenges require solutions driven by innovation, technology and a global perspective. Singapore and Israel place great emphasis on these parameters.

Despite our numerous differences, Singapore can draw inspiration from Israel's spirit and resolve to be self-reliant, fuelled by its most important resource: the wits of its people. We can look forward to continue expanding our ties in the economic, R&D and technology sectors. Together, Singapore and Israel can better overcome common challenges and seize shared opportunities.

Lieutenant-General (Retired) Winston Choo is Ambassador of the Republic of Singapore to the State of Israel.

Celebrating the Israel–Singapore Golden Jubilee: Working Towards Continued Partnership

Simona Halperin

In 2019, Israel and Singapore celebrate 50 years of diplomatic relations, friendship and collaboration that go back to the days when Israel and Singapore were two young countries. The bilateral relations are rooted in the shared values and challenges of the two young nations facing similar challenges — geo-strategic as well as economic, such as the lack of natural resources. For many years, it was a widely known, yet unspoken, secret that the beginning of our close relations was the Israeli response to Singapore's request for assistance and advice in building the Singapore Armed Forces. It was only in the year 2000, when the biography of founding Prime Minister Lee Kuan Yew, *From Third World to First: The Singapore Story 1965–2000*, was published that the 30-year-old secret was made public: Israel helped to develop the Singapore Armed Forces. Late Brigadier-General Yaakov (Jack) Elazari, then a colonel in the Israel Defense Forces (IDF), headed the secret Israeli military mission sent to train and build up the Singapore army, and is remembered in the book *Not Born in Singapore: Fifty Personalities who Shaped the Nation*.

Despite the establishment of full diplomatic relations since 1969, it took time for both countries to take those relations out of the shadows. It was only in April 1986 that President Wee Kim Wee made the first presidential visit from Singapore to Israel, followed by Israeli President Chaim Herzog's reciprocal visit to Singapore a few months later as part of an Asia tour. The strong negative reactions in the region following the visits are probably part of the reason why it took almost another 30 years before Singapore and Israel could receive official mutual visits from sitting prime ministers. In April 2016, Singapore's Prime Minister Lee Hsien Loong made his first official visit to Israel, followed by a visit by Israeli Prime Minister Benjamin Netanyahu to Singapore in February 2017.

Despite the lack of public fanfare, the two countries have been quietly working together. In fact, the appointment of Dr Shuki Gleitman as the Honorary Consul-General of Singapore in Israel in 1999, as well as the appointment of Lieutenant-General (Retired) Winston Choo Wee Leong as the non-resident Ambassador of Singapore to Israel in 2005 marked meaningful steps in the strengthening of bilateral relations.

Several mutual visits took place over the years. In late 1993, then-Israeli Prime Minister Yitzhak Rabin made a short visit to Singapore, following his visit to Indonesia to meet President Suharto, and invited Lee Kuan Yew, then Singapore's senior minister, to visit Israel. Senior Minister Lee led an education and economic delegation to Israel in May 1994. Meeting with Prime Minister Rabin, Foreign Minister Shimon Peres and the business leadership in Israel, Lee called for greater co-operation in the economic and business spheres. In 2015, then-President Reuven (Rubi) Rivlin represented the State of Israel to pay respects at Lee's funeral. But it was not until April 2016 that Prime Minister Lee Hsien Loong arrived in Israel, making it the first ever, historic official visit by a sitting Singapore prime minister to Israel. The visit was a significant step in "outing" the 50-year partnership between the two nations that grew wide and deep, spanning areas such as education, science, economy, technological collaboration, arts and culture.

Indeed, both Israel and Singapore are small in population (Israel's population is close to nine million while Singapore's is close to six million). While facing the challenges of being small in physical size and population, as well as lacking natural resources (though Israel will benefit from recently discovered natural gas), both countries compensated by having the best asset of all: human capital.

Both founding prime ministers David Ben-Gurion in Israel and Lee Kuan Yew in Singapore decided to devote significant resources to building an education system, realising that education is not only the source of prosperity and a successful economy, but also the strongest enabler for personal progress. That is especially so in a multi-ethnic society, consisting of people coming from various corners of the world (as is the case in both Singapore and Israel).

It is not surprising, therefore, that Prime Minister Lee Hsien Loong's first stop in Israel was the Hebrew University of Jerusalem, where he witnessed the signing of three agreements with the Hebrew University, and where the university conferred upon him an honorary doctorate.

Upon receiving the honorary doctorate, Mr Lee said:

> *Our relations have expanded much further, beyond defence and security, although those security ties remain. Our companies are very active in exploring opportunities in both countries. We collaborate in technology and in R&D (research and development). The Singapore–Israel Industrial Research & Development Foundation (SIIRD) has funded about 150 projects over the last 20 years, providing US$170 million in funding. Our universities and research institutes have regular exchanges, including with the Hebrew University. We have just witnessed the signing of three agreements — one with the National Research Foundation to manage Hebrew University's research in Singapore, one with the National University of Singapore, and one with the Nanyang Technological University, reaffirming the parties' commitment to deepen research collaboration. I hope we can build on these foundations to grow our relations further.*[1]

---

[1] For the full speech, see the website of the Prime Minister's Office: https://www.pmo.gov.sg/Newsroom/pm-lee-hsien-loong-hebrew-university-18-april-2016.

Indeed, this collaboration in education touches all areas of academic research and rose to new levels under the Share-Create agenda established in 2011, with two programmes — one covering medicine and biomedical science, another looking at nanomaterials for energy and water management.

The collaboration in biomedicine brings Israel's Start-up Nation culture of translational research and entrepreneurism to Singapore's research community, and has already resulted in major breakthroughs: Israeli and Singaporean researchers discovered an FDA-approved drug that can stop flesh-eating bacteria; another group of researchers reached a breakthrough against dengue fever with a dengue antibody discovery.

The collaboration in nanomaterial research has already seen scientific impact with 60 patents registered, which the team hopes will lead to more licensing and spin-offs. To date, the programme has initiated two spin-off companies and over 300 papers published during phase one alone in scientific journals, including *Nature Chemistry, Nature Materials,* and *Advanced Functional Materials*, among others.

In the healthcare sector, it is worth mentioning a few areas where the Singapore system is based on the Israeli model, experience and best practices. For haematology, or more specifically in the areas of leukaemia and bone marrow transplants, Professor Shimon Slavin, head of the bone marrow transplant unit at Hadassa Medical Center in Jerusalem, came to Singapore to perform two bone marrow transplants for two children, and shared experiences and techniques with his Singaporean colleagues. In the area of trauma, mass casualties, and the management of multiple trauma victims, Singapore's National University Health System and the medical sector are consulting Professor Avraham Rivkind, head of the Division of Emergency Medicine & Shock Trauma Unit at Hadassah Medical Center, who is introducing lessons from Israel in building up a trauma system for managing real-time incidents.

The Israel–Singapore academic and educational collaboration goes beyond research: Israel and Singapore share best practices in the education of gifted children as well as children with special needs. At the higher education level, dozens of university students from Singapore go to Israel every year for a six-month internship in an Israeli technology company or start-up, while attending a specialised programme on new venture creation or business innovation at Tel Aviv University or the Interdisciplinary Center (IDC) in Herzliya. The students participating in the programme enjoy exposure to a vibrant start-up ecosystem, providing the perfect meeting point for students from the smart nation of Singapore to be exposed to — and enriched by — the Start-up Nation's innovation culture.

In today's world, economic progress lies within collaboration and friendship among countries to facilitate an effective transformation. This is the aim of the SIIRD, which has existed since 1997.

As one of the global players, Singapore has always shown strong economic stature by being able to transform itself in the last 50 years. Despite the lack of natural resources to support its growing population, the country has always demonstrated a good capacity for handling its economy with agility. Singapore is now a thriving metropolis with an estimated gross domestic product (GDP) per capita of US$57,714, a far cry from its GDP of US$516 per capita in 1965.

Israel, on the other hand, is the gateway to the West and has been the staging ground for innovation and industrial research for more than a century. The World Economic Forum (WEF) Competitive Rankings Report 2018 ranked the country 20th with a macroeconomic stability of 99.1 per cent. Israel also ranked on the WEF report as one of the most highly industrialised countries, capitalising on infrastructure and information and communications technology (ICT) adoption. It was also ranked number one in the World Bank report on R&D expenditure as a percentage of GDP, demonstrating innovation, development and creativity. The 2019 Bloomberg Innovation Index ranked Israel number one for venture capital investment per capita, and fifth for the most innovative country in the world.

The SIIRD is a co-operative effort between Enterprise Singapore (ESG) and the Israel Innovation Authority. It promotes, facilitates and supports joint industrial R&D collaboration between Singapore-based companies and Israel-based companies across industries, providing research grants and government funding. Through joint R&D collaboration and SIIRD's funding, companies have created new or enhanced products and technology, and shortened the time required to bring the new or enhanced products and technology into the market. In June 2019, Singapore Technologies became the first Singaporean company to sign a partnership agreement with the Israel Innovation Authority with the goal of identifying and scouting for Israeli start-ups in the fields of smart mobility, security, and environmental protection.

SIIRD also promotes research and development within Singapore and Israel by helping Singapore-based and Israel-based companies with R&D partner search, and providing up to US$1 million in funding for joint R&D projects. In just over 20 years, SIIRD has approved over 174 projects between Israeli and Singapore entities, with a total grant of US$87 million. It achieved the employment of approximately 2,250 research scientists and engineers from both countries, with a total research investment of more than US$220 million. Among the projects approved by SIIRD are cutting-edge technologies such as stem cell technologies, graphene-based super capacitors, an algae-based oral vaccine for fish, wealth management solutions, and parenting applications.

Economic co-operation between Israel and Singapore does not stop at research and development; the Tel Aviv Stock Exchange (TASE) and the Singapore Exchange (SGX) entered into a partnership to focus on growing capital raising opportunities for companies, particularly in the technology sector. For the first time, Israeli and Singaporean companies are able to raise funds on both markets simultaneously through dual-listing (simultaneous initial public offerings on both exchanges). The two stock exchanges started to work together to support technology and healthcare companies that are looking to tap the capital markets, in order to fund their growth plans in Asia and globally. Major Singaporean companies, from Temasek Holdings (both with direct investments in and through acquisition of Israeli companies, as well as via venture capital funds Vertex and Red Dot Capital), to Singtel and ST Engineering have already discovered the potential of investing and collaborating with Israel, particularly in Israeli technology companies — from start-ups to mature tech companies.

To mark the first anniversary of the partnership, SGX, together with TASE and the Embassy of Israel in Singapore, organised a conference to introduce ground-breaking Israeli tech companies to Singapore. They shared the innovative thinking and unique approach to addressing challenges that have led Israel to thrive and become a technology powerhouse. The conference introduced potential investment opportunities in Israeli companies and allowed Asian investors to understand how Israel can be a new investment destination.

The economic section of the Israeli embassy also organises visits for business delegations of Israeli companies in Singapore, and for Singaporean companies visiting Israel. With over twenty such delegations in both directions every year, Israel and Singapore enjoy a significant and constant growth of their bilateral economic relations. This growth is reflected not only in measurable bilateral trade in goods of over US$2 billion in 2018 — more than five times the trade volume during founding Prime Minister Lee Kuan Yew's visit in 1994 — but also in the growing collaboration in services, including in areas such as fintech, mobility, smart transport, cybersecurity, energy, smart city and communications, just to name a few of the projects in recent years.

Beyond educational and economic co-operation, Israel and Singapore collaborate on the cultural front too. Since 1992, the Israel Film Festival, a project initiated by Ms Irit Lilian, then-Israeli Deputy Chief of Mission, has traditionally taken place in late August. The festival (held for the 27th time in August 2019) has become the annual flagship cultural event of Israel in Singapore, showcasing carefully selected feature films and providing viewers not only a diverse reflection of Israel, but also enriching the Singaporean audience with an authentic and real view of Israeli culture and society. The films tell stories of a vibrant, conflicted, modern society that is grappling with issues that are relatable to the audience in Singapore.

In 2015, the crown jewel of Israeli culture, the Israel Philharmonic Orchestra, along with Maestro Zubin Mehta, visited Singapore for the first time to perform a one-night-only concert. It was the State of Israel's tribute to the Republic's 50th anniversary. The success of that tour saw the orchestra revisiting Singapore in 2016. Israeli dance, theatre and musical groups also participate regularly in festivals in Singapore, and Israeli films are represented at all major film festivals in Singapore.

In 2019, to mark this very special year of the golden jubilee of diplomatic relations between Singapore and Israel, the Embassy of Israel in Singapore and a team of devoted Israeli volunteers organised the inaugural Tikkun Olam Makers (TOM) MakeAthon in June. The goal of the event was to come up with affordable solutions to challenges faced by persons with special needs. *Tikkun olam* is a Hebrew phrase that means "mending the world". TOM embodies the Israeli and Jewish value of *tikkun olam* by harnessing technology to serve the community and focusing on people with special needs. Bringing Israeli mentors and Singaporean volunteers together to design solutions for "need-knowers" was the best way of celebrating Singapore and Israel's 50th anniversary of diplomatic relations.

The core idea that each of us has a responsibility to use our talents to benefit society at large and to serve the people around us was remarkably displayed at the three-day event. The teams — comprising those with special needs and volunteers with different areas of expertise — worked together to devise simple yet innovative and cost-effective solutions for day-to-day challenges faced by those with special needs. The solutions devised will be uploaded to the global TOM website, and will be available — open source, free of charge — to anyone around the world suffering from similar challenges to download and replicate at the nearest available maker space or 3D printer. The solutions designed included:

- A lightweight prosthesis for someone with no hands;
- A lightweight retractable cane for the visually impaired;
- A mobile app to help people with Down's syndrome commute independently, while allowing their caregivers to stay in touch and track their travel;
- A hot plate with an audio guide for the visually impaired;

• A device to allow someone with muscular dystrophy to remotely unlock and open a door.

To commemorate the 50th anniversary of diplomatic relations between Singapore and Israel, Singapore Post Limited (SingPost), in collaboration with Israel Postal Company, jointly released an Israel–Singapore joint stamp issue. Singapore's Minister for Foreign Affairs Vivian Balakrishnan and I, in my capacity as Ambassador of Israel to Singapore, unveiled it on 8 May 2019 as part of Israel's 71st Independence Day celebrations. The joint stamp issue features flowers and birds native to both countries, symbolising the shared values and friendship between the two young nations.

Featured on the Singaporean stamp are flowers commonly found across the Republic's streets and parks, including the pigeon orchid, golden shower, bougainvillea and ixora. The design is a nod to Singapore's unique reputation as a garden city. Likewise, the Israeli stamp features several species of flowers found in Israel, including the anemone, cyclamen, senecio and the narcissus. These colourful flowers are synonymous with Israel's landscape at different times of the year. Both stamps also feature a species of bird associated with each state. The crimson sunbird, a small and active bird with the males sporting a red plumage, represents Singapore. Israel's national bird, the hoopoe, is featured facing the sunbird on both stamps.

The beautiful array of flowers is a reflection of how both of our countries celebrate the diversity found within each nation, as well as the grounded and robust friendship and collaboration between the two nations. The birds and butterflies featured are a symbolic representation that the sky is the limit for the unique partnership between Israel and Singapore. The joint stamp issue speaks volumes of the rich history and collaboration between the two countries.

In 50 years of diplomatic relations, and an even longer period of friendship and collaboration, Israel and Singapore have carved their place in the international arena. Both young nations are "punching above their weights" in economic development, supported by a wide network of international trade relations, innovation and entrepreneurship, as well as excellence in education and a strong emphasis on technology. As much as the relations build on similarities, they are enriched by the differences between the two cultures. Singapore's Confucian culture of respect for teachers and seniors, as well as long-term planning and execution abilities, is almost the exact opposite of the Israeli character of challenging conventions by thinking outside the box, which leads to creative, innovative and non-traditional solutions. However, it is when Singapore's ordered and meticulous performance meets the chaotic Israeli nature that the synergy of collaboration reaches its peak and sparks fly.

Fun Facts

- The Night Safari in Singapore uses Israeli night vision technology.

- Schools in Israel adopted the Singaporean method of maths teaching, while Singapore learnt Israeli creative investigative teaching methods.

- Both the ArtScience Museum in Singapore and Yad Vashem — the World Holocaust Remembrance Center in Israel — were designed by Israeli architect Moshe Safdie.

- Singapore Airlines sold planes to Israel's national airline, El-Al.

- The tallest building in Singapore is the Tanjong Pagar Centre at 290m (64 floors). The tallest building in Israel is Azrieli at 238m (61 floors).

- National Service is mandatory in both Singapore and Israel, though in Israel it is also mandatory for girls.

- *Krav Maga* is an Israeli martial art, created by — and for — the Israeli army. It literally translates to "contact battle". It uses very simple principles of self-defence that allow every man and woman, girl and boy to feel strong, confident, and able to defend themselves if facing an attack. You can receive Israeli *krav maga* training in Singapore.

- *Assam pedas*, the famous Singaporean dish of sour and spicy fish in red *sambal* sauce, is similar to *chraime* (המיירח), an Israeli Sephardic dish of fish in spicy tomato sauce.

- Walking around Singapore, one can find streets named after Jewish families, such as Zion Road, Frankel Avenue, Nassim Road and Elias Road.

- The first Chief Minister of Singapore, David Marshall, was Jewish.

- Albert Einstein, Nobel laureate in physics famous for his e=mc^2 equation and his Special Theory of Relativity, visited Singapore in November 1922 to raise funds for the building of the Hebrew University in Jerusalem, Israel.

- Israeli vlogger Nuseir Yassin (commonly known by his media name Nas for his multimillion follower vlog *NAS Daily*) moved to Singapore in April 2019, making it his home base.

Simona Halperin was Israel's Ambassador to Singapore and East Timor from 2017 to 2019.

Reflections on Singapore–Israel Relations

George Yeo

As a Secondary One student, looking at the *Time* magazine map comparing the military forces of Israel with those of the surrounding Arab countries in early 1967, I feared for Israel's ability to defend itself. Egyptian President Gamal Nasser had blockaded the Straits of Tiran, which was *casus belli*. War was inevitable. As it happened, the Six Day War saw the mighty Israel Defense Forces (IDF) vanquishing Arab military forces with seeming ease. I followed the battles day by day and became familiar with exotic places like Sharm el-Sheikh, el-Arish and Quneitra. Golda Meir, Moshe Dayan, Abba Eban, Ezer Weizman and Israel Tal became legends in my mind.

As a young teenager preparing for National Service, the Six Day War gave me hope that the young Singapore Armed Forces (SAF) could also be credible. After separation from Malaysia in August 1965, one of Singapore's first acts of nationhood was to pick up the gun, without which sovereignty had no meaning. Lee Kuan Yew asked India's Prime Minister Jawaharlal Nehru and Nasser for help to build up our defence forces, but both declined. He then turned to Israeli Prime Minister David Ben-Gurion, who agreed. Israel's prowess during the Six Day War gave a huge boost to the SAF's morale. We had found the right advisers. Vacationing with my family in the Cameron Highlands at the end of 1965, my eldest brother reported that Lee Kuan Yew had announced the introduction of compulsory military service. A certain excitement gripped us boys. For many Chinese families, the idea of becoming soldiers was foreign. Just as good iron is not used for making nails, good men do not become soldiers. In order to overcome the deep cultural resistance to military careers, Lee Kuan Yew and Dr Goh Keng Swee introduced an SAF Scholarship scheme. 'Scholar-officer' is a term peculiar to Singapore and a source of confusion to foreigners. For years, Israeli military advisers were deeply sceptical that "scholars" could provide the strong leadership a strong defence force required.

In 1969, Singapore established diplomatic relations with Israel. Our relations before that were discreet for fear of offending our Muslim neighbours. National servicemen were told that the military advisers were from Mexico. In May 1969, racial riots broke out in Malaysia and spilled into Singapore. Concerned that the upsurge of Malay nationalism in Malaysia would become a problem for Singapore, a political decision was taken to roll out AMX-13 tanks on National Day, when the Malaysian Prime Minister was a guest. Our tank units were hardly ready for combat at that time, but a point was made. Openly recognising Israel that year was part of the same calculus.

In 1973, I went up to Cambridge as an SAF scholar. During Sunday Mass on a cold October morning at Fisher Hall, a female student prayed for peace in the Middle East. War had broken out again in the region. Catching Israel by surprise, Egyptian forces crossed the Suez Canal and made rapid gains under the cover of Soviet surface-to-air missiles. It was only after Ariel Sharon found a point of weakness in the Egyptian battlefront, broke through, crossed the Suez Canal and systematically destroyed surface-to-air missile batteries on the other side that the Israeli Air Force was able to unfurl its wings again. After the ceasefire, Saudi Arabia weighed in and imposed an oil embargo on those who supported Israel. This first oil shock affected Singapore's economy severely. Singapore was forced to recalibrate. The SAF told its Israeli military advisers to take off their uniforms. They became consultants. However, military relations with Israel continued to strengthen.

As a captain in late 1979, I was suddenly posted from Army Signals to the Air Plans Department of the Republic of Singapore Air Force (RSAF), which was expanding rapidly. In 1980, I was thrilled to be included in Defence Minister Howe Yoon Chong's visit to Israel. In the delegation were Second Permanent Secretary Philip Yeo, Director of Security and Intelligence Eddie Teo and Deputy Chief of General Staff Tan Chin Tiong. We visited an Israeli Air Force base, the Golan Heights, Masada and Jerusalem, and met Israel Tal and Ezer Weizman. Minister Howe had a private meeting with Israeli Prime Minister Menachem Begin. Israeli Air Force Commander David Ivry and Israeli Defence Ministry Secretary-General Joseph Maayan arranged the detailed programme for our visit. It left an indelible impression on me. When David Ivry and Joseph Maayan visited Singapore separately in the months afterwards, I was asked by Philip Yeo to be their bag carrier.

David Ivry came to know Singapore well. At a personal level, he became like an uncle to me. When I became head of Air Plans, he sent an adviser to help me at the Israeli Air Force's (IAF) expense. Colonel Yaakov Gal, a Mirage pilot who flew many sorties during the Six Day War, was hands-on, constantly prodding us to change and improve. I must have visited Israel ten times in three years. After the Lebanon War in 1982, during which the IAF had complete dominance of the sky, I was given detailed briefings and shown cockpit film clips of air-to-air combat with the Syrian Air Force. David Ivry had insisted on taking part in a bombing mission to lead by example. His staff told me that the entire mission was planned around keeping him safe. Commanders leading from the front was a core principle of the IDF. I developed a healthy respect for the IDF and learned much from their successes and setbacks. Some of their experiences were profoundly relevant to us; others, less so. David Ivry felt strongly that the commander of the RSAF should always be a fighter pilot but we were not always able to achieve this. One day, while drawing up the layout for operational planning in the Air Force Command Post, Yaakov Gal objected to having different rooms for the planning teams. I had noticed this arrangement in their command post.

He replied that Israelis constantly and loudly argued with one another and needed separate spaces for a bit of quiet. In Singapore's case, we were less boisterous and could do with more debate and interaction.

I became an ardent student of the history and condition of Israel and the Jewish people. During my visits, I always made time to visit places, meet people and buy books. Yaakov, his wife, Amalia, and their children became my close family friends. Through him, David Ivry and others, I had a sense of the intensity of daily life in Israel. Once, on our way to the Dead Sea, I asked Yaakov if he could make a detour for us to see Jericho (at that time still under Israeli occupation). He said, sure, and cheerfully asked his son, who was sitting next to him, if his pistol was in the glove compartment. Sitting at the back, my wife and I looked at each other somewhat disturbed. A foreigner visiting Israel is often taken aback by the level of security. It takes a while to get used to loaded assault rifles slung on the shoulders of young soldiers pointing at our feet in hotel lifts. David Ivry had a son who was killed when the F-16 he was flying crashed during a training flight.

As a Cabinet minister in different portfolios, I endeavoured to foster close ties with Israel. After the Oslo Accords in 1993, when the prospects for peace in the Middle East had improved so much, a senior Israeli official told me that it was possible to envisage driving from Cairo to Damascus in the not-too-distant future. At Davos in 1999, Israeli Trade Minister Ran Cohen asked for a meeting. He wanted to visit Singapore with his Palestinian counterpart, and for the three of us to visit our Indonesian counterpart in Batam. Singapore's economic co-operation with Indonesia should have been an inspiration to Israeli-Palestinian co-operation. My heart leapt and, on returning home, I proceeded to make preparations. Unfortunately, within a few months, the Second Intifada broke out and the hope became a pipe dream.

Israel's relations with its neighbours are fraught. Former US Secretary of State Henry Kissinger always argued that grand solutions were not possible. One should instead take small steps which open up possibilities for the future, and let history find its course gradually. While there are some similarities between Israel's circumstances and Singapore's, the politics of Southeast Asia are happily much more benign than the politics in the Middle East. Former US Trade Representative Charlene Barshefsky compared Singapore to Israel when we launched negotiations for the US–Singapore Free Trade Area at the end of 2000. I was alarmed and quickly corrected her that while she could compare Israel to Singapore, not the other way around, please.

Over the past 50 years, Singapore's relationship with Israel has deepened and broadened. There is mutual respect and affection. From time to time, Israel takes issue with Singapore's lack of support at the United Nations and other international forums. It could not be otherwise because Singapore has friendly relations with Palestine, all of Israel's neighbours, and with Iran. We are also firm in our support for a two-state solution. Once, while visiting Syria, after receiving intelligence reports that Israel had made contact with Hamas, I met a senior Hamas representative to get a better sense of their perspective. I made clear our own. He knew Singapore had good relations with Israel. Talking about Gaza, I remarked that it was half the size of Singapore, with less than half its population. He listened intently when I said that a country's development depended ultimately on the quality of the people, not on the size of the country. The Israeli Foreign Ministry was not happy that the meeting took place, but understood our intentions. I also took the opportunity to discuss Israel with Sheikh Yusef al-Qaradawi, an Egyptian Islamic theologian in Doha, in 2004 and Iranian Grand Ayatollah Mahmoud Hashemi Shahroudi in Qom in 2010. When I visited Israel as Foreign Minister in 2007, I asked Deputy Prime Minister Avigdor Lieberman bluntly whether Israel's settlement policy would not make a future two-state outcome impossible. He replied without hesitation that Israeli settlements were dismantled in Gaza and could be dismantled elsewhere if the political agreement called for it.

For years, Lee Kuan Yew avoided visiting Israel in order to maintain balance in our relationship with the Arab world. He left Israel to Dr Goh Keng Swee, who built up the defence relationship and had a shrewd understanding of the Israeli situation. A visiting Israeli dignitary once lamented to him the fractiousness of Israeli domestic politics. Dr Goh guffawed, remarking that, under threat, the Israelis were solidly united, and that was what mattered. In 1993, Israeli Prime Minister Yitzhak Rabin visited Singapore after the first Oslo Accord. He called on Lee Kuan Yew and, in a pro forma way, knowing Lee's longstanding policy of not going to Israel, invited him to make an official visit now that there was a peace agreement. I was at the meeting and could see the surprise on Rabin's face when the invitation was immediately accepted. The Singapore Foreign Ministry was surprised, too. Rabin hosted Lee's only visit to Israel in May 1994. A year and a half later, Rabin was assassinated.

So many personal friendships now bind our two countries together. On my visit to Israel in 2007, David Ivry arranged for my wife and I to attend the IAF wings parade at Hatzerim. It was a moving experience. Not only was it attended by the Prime Minister, the Defence Minister and the IDF Chief of General Staff, but many retired air force commanders and senior officers were also present. I think we were among very few foreign guests that day. My wife and I felt like close friends invited to a family gathering.

In 2005, I was invited to speak at the American Jewish Committee Annual Gala Dinner in Washington, DC. It was a rowdy affair. Several senior IDF officers from a visiting delegation attended in uniform. On the podium were the flags of the United States, Israel and Singapore. I recalled the critical contribution that Israel made to the build-up of the SAF in the early years of independence and talked about the implications of the rise of China and the rest of Asia on Israel and the Middle East. In the Arab world, there were individuals who saw Israel as a latter-day Crusader state supported by the West which would eventually be extruded from the region again. Between Israel and the Arab countries, there were many reasons for the mutual distrust of one another's promises. Seen within the existing geopolitical frame of the Arab world versus the West, there appeared no end to the cycle of distrust and violence. The re-emergence of Asia would enlarge the frame. One could begin to re-imagine the future against a more distant past, when the Levant was a prosperous region connecting Asia to Europe. Israel should therefore look increasingly to Asia and build relations, especially with China, the Association of Southeast Asian Nations and India. As it does so, Singapore's contribution to Israel in the 21st century will become more important. Our 50th anniversary celebration is therefore not only of the past, but for the future.

George Yeo was Singapore's Minister for Foreign Affairs from 2004 to 2011.

A Mexican *Fandango* with a Poisonous Shrimp

Peter Ho

Introduction

The defence ties between Singapore and Israel are almost as old as independent Singapore. Arguably, this unusual partnership was the foundation upon which the larger bilateral relationship has been built.

But for many years, it was shrouded in secrecy.

To this day, little has been written about the Singapore–Israel defence relationship despite its significance. This reticence is derived from the reality of Singapore's neighbourhood. The state visit of then-Israeli President Chaim Herzog to Singapore in 1986 sparked demonstrations — and political remonstrations — in both Malaysia and Indonesia. This experience would have reinforced in the minds of policymakers in Singapore that the bilateral relationship with Israel — above all, the sensitive defence relationship — had to be managed discreetly in order to preserve and protect the substance. So all these years, while Singapore has not denied that it has close defence links with Israel, at the same time, it has eschewed speaking openly about them and revealed few details.

Indeed, this low-key approach was adopted when the first team of military advisers from the Israel Defense Forces (IDF) visited Singapore in 1965, soon after Singapore's separation from Malaysia. To disguise their presence, they were famously described as "Mexicans". In his memoirs, Lee Kuan Yew remarked that they looked "swarthy enough",[1] presumably because of their tough life in training and operations under the hot Levantine sun. Since then, Singapore's links with the Israeli defence establishment have grown in breadth and depth. A close relationship between two very different systems emerged. If the Israelis were "Mexicans", then perhaps the active and lively way that Singapore engaged Israel on the defence front could be described as a Mexican *fandango*.[2]

The Beginning

To understand the roots of this Mexican *fandango*, we need to go back to 1965, when Singapore separated from Malaysia. Few then gave Singapore much chance of surviving on its own, let alone succeeding. With the unexpected and unwanted divorce, Singapore lost its economic hinterland in Malaysia. A communist insurgency was barely over. President Soekarno's Indonesia was still waging an armed confrontation — *Konfrontasi* — against the "neo-colonialist" creation of Malaysia, and Singapore was not spared. The Vietnam War was growing in intensity.

These were not propitious beginnings for the newly independent state of Singapore. It was a very parlous situation that convinced the Singaporean leadership of the imperative to rapidly build up a credible — and independent — defence capability. It was an existential priority from day one.

It did not take rocket science to figure out that Singapore's defences were in a bad state. At independence, Singapore had only two under-strength infantry battalions, with more than half of the soldiers Malaysians. There was an ageing wooden gunboat, and not a single aircraft — nothing that could pass for either a navy or an air force. Although the British maintained a large military presence in Singapore and Malaysia, political pressure was growing

---

[1] Lee Kuan Yew, *From Third World to First: The Singapore Story, 1965–2000* (New York: HarperCollins Publishers, 2000), p. 31.
[2] A *fandango* is a lively dance between couples. It traces its origins to Spain.

back in London to cut its military presence east of the Suez. Singapore had to assume that the British military presence would be withdrawn at some point in time.[3] Singapore had to be able to defend itself. Reflecting this determination, Lee said in 1966 that in a world where the big fish eat small fish and the small fish eat shrimp, Singapore must become a *poisonous shrimp*. It may have been bravado then, but the poisonous shrimp metaphor staked out the beginnings of a defence strategy of deterrence that would eventually be embraced by Singapore.[4] So, the task was clear-cut, yet overwhelming — to build an army virtually from scratch, and quickly.

Dr Goh Keng Swee, then Finance Minister, volunteered to lead the effort, although Lee wryly noted that all Goh knew of military matters had been learnt as a corporal in the British-led Singapore Volunteer Corps until it surrendered to the Japanese in February 1942.[5] A small team under the leadership of Goh was hastily assembled to form the new Ministry of Interior and Defence, combining into one ministry what is today divided into the Ministry of Defence and the Ministry of Home Affairs.

With a small population and limited resources, Singapore could not afford a large professional army. Initially, the government tried to get round the problem of cost by establishing a part-time volunteer "territorial" army. It created the People's Defence Force (PDF) soon after independence.[6] But, truth be told, the government was not confident of getting enough volunteers,

---

[3] In July 1967, Britain announced that it would withdraw its troops from Singapore by the mid-1970s. But six months later, the deadline was brought forward to 1971.

[4] Tim Huxley, in *Defending the Lion City* (Sydney: Allen & Unwin, 2000), describes it as Singapore's *declaratory strategy* up to the 1980s.

[5] Lee, *Third World*, p. 30.

[6] The PDF was established as a part-time paramilitary defence force following the enactment of the People's Defence Force Act 1965 through an Act of Parliament passed on 30 December 1965. The PDF's predecessor was the Singapore Volunteer Corps (SVC) which Goh Keng Swee had served in. The PDF was conceived as a reserve combat unit to supplement the regular Singapore Army in the defence of Singapore. As a volunteer force, the PDF was considered as the fastest way for the nation to build up a credible defence force before the conscription-based National Service was introduced in March 1967.

especially as the majority Chinese population had a cultural aversion to service in the military. It was not a sustainable model.

Seeking Help

As he did with the Singapore economy, Goh's approach to defence was "to seek good advice" from those who had trodden the path before. Singapore had already approached Egypt and India — both members of the Non-Aligned Movement, like Singapore — for help in building up its defences. After a few weeks of waiting, India and Egypt congratulated Singapore on its independence, but did not offer military aid. It was only then that Lee gave the go-ahead to approach Israel for help. However, he instructed Goh to keep it from the public eye for as long as possible, so as not to arouse negative reactions, either domestically or in the region.[7]

First Contact

Goh had already been impressed by Israel's defence system during his first visit to the country in January 1959, when he was Minister for Finance.[8] Israel is a small country like Singapore, but located in a hostile region. It had been among the first to recognise Singapore. Lee recounted how, after Singapore's separation from Malaysia, Goh contacted Mordecai Kidron, the former Israeli Ambassador to Thailand. Kidron then flew to Singapore with a Mossad representative, Hezi Carmel, with instructions to offer military assistance. Kidron met Goh, as well as Lee, whom he knew from earlier encounters.[9] Carmel said that Goh had told them that only Israel, a small country with a strong army, could help Singapore to build a "small, dynamic army".[10]

---

[7] Lee, *Third World*, p. 31.

[8] Tan Siok Sun, *Goh Keng Swee: A Portrait* (Singapore: Editions Didier Millet, 2007), p. 128.

[9] Kidron had met Lee Kuan Yew when he visited Singapore on a few occasions between 1962 and 1963 to ask to open an Israeli consulate in Singapore, which was to join Malaysia. But Tunku Abdul Rahman, the Prime Minister of Malaysia, did not agree to this.

[10] Amnon Barzilai, "A Deep, Dark, Secret Love Affair", *Haaretz*, 16 July 2004.

Kidron would have reported his visit to his boss, Golda Meir, who was then Israel's Foreign Minister. Meir had already met Lee at various international conferences, and admired him as an outstanding Asian leader. She wanted to be helpful. So the then-IDF Chief of General Staff (and future Prime Minister of Israel), Lieutenant-General Yitzhak Rabin, together with his deputy and Head of the Operations Directorate (and future President of Israel), Major-General Ezer Weizman, assigned Major-General Rehavam Ze'evi the task of assisting Singapore.[11]

Ze'evi was then the IDF's Deputy Head of the Operations Directorate. He had the intriguing nickname "Gandhi". Ze'evi was despatched to Singapore in October 1965 to meet Goh under conditions of great secrecy.

The Brown Book

During his visit to Singapore, ever the military professional, Ze'evi travelled incognito by taxi around Singapore to familiarise himself with the terrain and the ground conditions.[12] Upon his return to Tel Aviv, he assembled his team, which included Meir Amit, then director of Mossad. They developed a masterplan for the build-up of the Singapore Armed Forces (SAF). This masterplan was called *The Brown Book*. Ze'evi had it ready within a month, and translated it into English two months later.

The Brown Book was broad in scope. It covered strategy and doctrine. But at its core was the fundamental assessment that the only viable solution for Singapore was to build a citizen army of conscripts, trained and led by a small regular force. To this end, it proposed the establishment of an "Officer Training School" to produce this corps of professional leaders. Citizen-soldiers would form the backbone of the citizen army, so that in an emergency, the entire nation could be mobilised under arms. *The Brown Book* detailed a masterplan to put this concept into effect. It envisaged, among other things,

---

[11] Tan, *Goh Keng Swee*, p. 129.

[12] Pang Eng Fong and Arnoud De Meyer, eds., *Within & Without: Singapore in the World, the World in Singapore* (Singapore: Singapore Management University, 2016), p. 107.

the army's expansion to 12 battalions within a decade, an objective that could only be achieved through conscription.

Soon after, the Singapore and Israeli governments signed a one-page agreement, which stated simply that Israel would provide defence advisers to Singapore. They would be given their equivalent Israeli salaries, plus board and lodging.[13] Indeed, these terms proved to be very generous on Israel's part, as Singapore benefited enormously from the priceless advice of the Israelis.

A small group of seven Israeli advisers — or "Mexicans", if you will — led by Colonel Yaakov "Jack" Elazari arrived in Singapore in November 1965. Prior to their departure, they had met Rabin, who told the team:

> *"I want you to remember several things. One, we are not going to turn Singapore into an Israeli colony. Your task is to teach them the military profession, to put them on their legs so they can run their own army. Your success will be if at a certain stage they will be able to take the wheel and run the army by themselves. Second, you are not going there in order to command them but to advise them. And third, you are not arms merchants. When you recommend items to procure, use the purest professional military judgment. I want total disregard of their decision as to whether to buy here or elsewhere."[14]*

The team came with two suitcases containing 20 copies of *The Brown Book*.[15] They were followed by a team of six more advisers in December 1965.

The masterplan contained in *The Brown Book* was approved quickly. In February 1967, Lee announced the government's intention to introduce National Service. This was a crucial decision: to transform the fledgling Singapore military from a small force of regulars supplemented by volunteer reservists into a military force of citizen-soldiers based on conscription and long-term compulsory reservist service, as envisaged in *The Brown Book*. The

---

[13] Tan, *Goh Keng Swee*, p. 130.
[14] Barzilai, "Love Affair".
[15] Pang & De Meyer, *Within & Without*, p. 107.

National Service (Amendment) Bill was introduced in Parliament.[16] There can be no doubt that the Israeli link profoundly influenced the development of the SAF, particularly in its early stages.[17] Of course, it did not end there. Indeed, *The Brown Book* was followed by *The Blue Book*, which dealt with the creation of the Ministry of Defence and the intelligence bodies.[18]

A Running Start

When Elazari landed in Singapore, like Ze'evi before him, he too familiarised himself with the terrain. Driving himself around the island, he kept an eye out for potential sites for the Officer Training School that had been proposed in *The Brown Book.* He eventually selected Pasir Laba, having earlier ruled out two islands north-east of the main island: Pulau Ubin and Pulau Tekong. Elazari made his recommendations to Goh. They were accepted, and led to the establishment of the Singapore Armed Forces Training Institute, or SAFTI.[19] The bulldozers quickly moved into Pasir Laba. Within a year, the construction of SAFTI was completed, based on plans from the Israeli Engineering Corps. It was an impressive feat, even if SAFTI was very basic in design and facilities, driven by the urgency to get the SAF up and running.

With SAFTI, the Israeli advisers were truly ready for business. Their first priority was to build up a pool of Singaporean instructors and commanders. In the parlance, they "trained the trainers". They insisted from the very start that the Singaporean officers were to learn from them so that they could take over as instructors as soon as possible. Every job they did was understudied by a Singaporean counterpart, from platoon commanders to company commanders, right up to the top position of director general staff. They even had the officer cadets write the instructional material. Lee

---

[16] The National Service (Amendment) Act was passed on 15 March 1967, making National Service (NS) compulsory for all 18-year-old male Singapore citizens and permanent residents.

[17] The Singapore Armed Forces Act 1972 was introduced to strengthen and improve the management of the nation's defence forces. The act unified the army, navy and air commands into a single force known as the Singapore Armed Forces, and established the Armed Forces Council.

[18] Barzilai, "Love Affair".

[19] Tan, Goh Keng Swee, p. 131.

observed that while the Americans had sent about 3,000 to 6,000 men in the first batch of military advisers to help President Ngo Dinh Diem build up the South Vietnamese army, the Israelis sent only 18 officers.[20]

Tough Training

To meet these urgent needs for instructors and commanders, police officers and former Singapore Volunteer Corps officers from British days were recruited into the SAF. Even civil servants and teachers, and some from the private sector, were roped into the effort and offered full-time appointments.[21]

But these early recruits were cut no slack. The Israelis demanded high standards from these pioneers because it was upon their shoulders that future generations of citizen-soldiers would be trained for the SAF.

The no-nonsense professional tone was set by the first course for officer cadets. It followed an IDF regimen, beginning each day with wake-up at 5.30am, followed by exercise and parade. Training started at 7.30am and ran till 1am the next day. It seems that the officer cadets complained about this tough schedule. A few days later, Elazari arrived at SAFTI with Goh, who told the cadets in no uncertain terms to follow instructions, "otherwise you will do double".[22]

Such rumblings never quite disappeared. I recall that when I was called up for National Service a few years later, in December 1972, there were dark whispers about the "Mexicans". Rumours were rife that they were actually Israelis. By then, of course, the IDF had acquired a fearsome reputation for its swift and decisive victory against Israel's Arab neighbours during the Six Day War. We heard that the Israeli training had been incorporated into the SAF syllabus, and the word going round was that it was extremely tough — and dangerous. Live ammunition was used, and occasionally, national servicemen were injured, even killed. Of course, this was all exaggeration and

---

[20] Lee, Third World, p. 42.

[21] Ibid.

[22] Barzilai, "Love Affair".

rumour-mongering in the hothouse of the early years of National Service. But I suspect that such rumours served a useful purpose, because it persuaded us in those days that our military training was to be taken very seriously.

The Israelis emphasised military skills and motivation. Lieutenant-Colonel Yehuda Golan, then commander of an IDF armoured division and part of the first team of Israeli advisers, recounted how he and Elazari tried to persuade Lee of the importance of motivation. They cited the defeat of the British Army by the Japanese Imperial Army in World War Two. They argued that the Japanese soldier was motivated because he was fighting for his emperor, who was God to him. The British soldier had little motivation because he was fighting thousands of kilometres from his home. According to Golan, these explanations about the spirit of combat and the importance of motivation persuaded Lee.[23]

Indeed, this must have made an impression on Lee, who later observed that the training methods adopted by the Israelis were the exact opposite of the British, who had built the First and Second Battalions, Singapore Infantry Regiment (1 SIR and 2 SIR).[24] He noted that "smartness on parade and military tattoo the SAF never learnt from the Israelis".[25] Perhaps with a tinge of ruefulness, he also noted that whatever spit and polish that the SAF had acquired would have come from British officers in charge of 1 SIR and 2 SIR in the early years, which was never quite purged from the system.

In under a year, apart from the officer cadet course, the Israeli team had also conducted a course for recruits, and for platoon commanders.[26]

---

[23] Barzilai, "Love Affair".

[24] The First and Second Battalions, Singapore Infantry Regiment, were formed in 1957 and 1962 respectively against the backdrop of self-government for Singapore. They were the first two battalions of what eventually became the SAF.

[25] Lee, Third World, p. 43.

[26] Barzilai, "Love Affair".

A Secret No More

On 16 July 1967, Zeévi, together with the other Israeli advisers, was invited by Goh to the commissioning parade of the first batch of 117 Singapore officer cadets who had completed their training at SAFTI. On Goh's instruction, they came in their IDF military uniforms. Goh then explained their presence. He said:

> *"You have heard of the Six Day War, which commenced on 5 June. Seated here with me today are part of the Israeli mission which has been advising us on how to build an army."*[27]

The "Mexicans" had been unmasked as Israelis. This revelation signalled that Singapore was now ready to deal with any military threat. With this disclosure coming after the Six Day War in June 1967, the deterrence message was clear: that since the SAF had been designed and trained by the Israelis, it would be a force to be reckoned with. Goh was staking out the parameters of the poisonous shrimp strategy.

Building Deterrence

However, it was not only through training that Singapore's poisonous shrimp strategy was being realised with the assistance of Israel. In great secrecy, Singapore purchased 72 AMX-13 light tanks from IDF surplus. To support this acquisition, the IDF trained the pioneer team of 36 SAF armour officers in its own armour school back in Israel, just as it had also begun training other military vocationalists from Singapore.

---

[27] Tan, *Goh Keng Swee*, p. 138.

Then the bombshell was dropped. On Singapore's National Day on 9 August 1969, 30 of these AMX-13 tanks rolled past the reviewing stand at the Padang.[28] With understatement, Lee wrote: "it had a dramatic effect ..."[29]

While some may have had reservations over the relevance of Israel's military experience to Singapore's tropical environment, there is no doubt that the IDF has been one of the most important influences on the development of the SAF. The "Mexicans" played a key role in the early years of the SAF, helping to establish its National Service system, its training system and its military organisation.

Equipping the SAF

Israel has also been a key source of defence equipment and technology. Although the Israelis remained faithful over the years to Rabin's injunction not to be "arms merchants", it was almost inevitable that Israeli weapons systems would soon begin to enter the inventory of the SAF. First, because the SAF was influenced by Israeli military doctrine, and, second, because the Israeli defence industry produced superior, and often battle-tested, weapons systems.

For example, it is not surprising that the Israeli emphasis on artillery in its military doctrine was mirrored by a similar emphasis in the SAF. Some of the earliest artillery in the SAF's inventory came from Israel — the Soltam 60mm, and the 81mm mortars. Two of three types of 155mm artillery that came into service in the SAF during the 1970s also came from Israel: the M-68s in 1971, and the M-71s in 1979. A dozen Soltam 160mm heavy mortars were also acquired in 1980.[30]

Indeed, the Israeli influence was felt beyond the Singapore Army. In 1967, the Israeli Navy destroyer *Eilat* was sunk by Russian-made Styx

---

[28] The Padang is an open field located in the central area of Singapore. It is of great historical significance and has been used as a venue for National Day Parades in some years. The first ever National Day Parade was held there in 1966.

[29] Lee, *Third World*, p. 40.

[30] Huxley, *Defending*, p. 130.

surface-to-surface missiles launched by Egyptian Navy missile boats. This disaster signalled a new era in naval combat — the deployment of missiles. In response, Israel Aircraft Industries (IAI) developed the Gabriel surface-to-surface missile, which then sank four Syrian warships in a naval encounter during the Yom Kippur War of 1973. By then, these Gabriel missiles were beginning to be deployed on Singapore's new 45-metre missile gunboats designed by Lürssen Werft, marking a significant upgrade of the nascent Maritime Command.[31]

Beyond a Poisonous Shrimp

By the end of the 1970s, the First Generation SAF had been established. National Service had been fully implemented. There was a corps of regular soldiers. There was a proper training pipeline that generated the citizen-soldiers for the SAF. Singapore had the beginnings of a defence industry, a basic engineering capability, the outline of the three division structure in the army, and a basic air defence capability.

Hence, by the early 1980s, Singapore started to look beyond the poisonous shrimp strategy and began to contemplate the task of building the Second Generation SAF (2G SAF), which would be better equipped and operating on more advanced military concepts. To this end, the Israelis provided reference, both for military concepts as well as equipping. For example, in the 1980s, the SAF became one of the earliest users of unmanned systems — a technology championed by the IDF — when it acquired the Scout Remotely-Piloted Vehicle (RPV) from IAI.[32]As the 2G SAF began to take shape, other more advanced systems were introduced into the SAF's inventory. The Singapore Navy acquired new missile corvettes, in which many of the sophisticated combat systems were of Israeli origin, including

---

[31] The missile gunboats were the most advanced in the inventory of the Maritime Command in the 1970s. The Maritime Command became the Republic of Singapore Navy in 1975, when the SAF established its component forces into three distinct services.

[32] In the mid-1990s, Singapore purchased about 40 Searcher UAVs from IAI to replace the Scout UAVs.

the Barak anti-missile missile system.[33] A complex upgrade programme for the whole F-5E/F fleet of the Republic of Singapore Air Force was launched in 1991 to improve interception capability. Elbit did the systems integration, which involved installing a more effective radar and an up-to-date navigation/attack system.[34]

By the turn of the century and at the start of the new millennium, the 2G SAF had been established. It was no longer just a poisonous shrimp, and would probably have been unrecognisable in many ways to the original team of Israeli advisers, but had Israeli influence embedded in its equipping and its operational concepts.

The Future of the Mexican *Fandango*

From the start of the 21 century, the SAF has begun to transform itself once again. Given the shrinking manpower pool, it has focused on maximising the use of the human resource by adopting new force multiplier concepts and technologies, transforming itself into what is today referred to as the 3G — or Third Generation — SAF.

As the SAF evolves, how will the defence relationship between Singapore and Israel change? It is clear that it will change in tandem. But what I think will remain constant is a deep respect on the Singapore side for the Israeli defence system and its professionalism, which, through the early efforts of the "Mexicans", is now part of the DNA of the SAF, and an abiding sense of gratitude towards Israel that it was a friend in need when Singapore's need was greatest.

Peter Ho, who headed Singapore's civil service from 2005 to 2010, was Permanent Secretary (Defence) from 2000 to 2004.

---

[33] Singapore was the launch customer of the Barak system, developed by IAI.
[34] Tim Huxley, *Defending the Lion City* (Sydney: Allen & Unwin, 2000), p. 143.

Manasseh Meyer, the patriarch of the Jewish community in Singapore in the late 1870s, was knighted for his contributions both in Singapore and overseas. Photo: Courtesy of National Archives of Singapore (NAS).

A view of Belle Vue House on Oxley Rise, Sir Manasseh Meyer's residence, in the 1980s. Photo: Goh Chong Chia Collection, courtesy of NAS.

Maghain Aboth Synagogue and the Jacob Ballas Centre on Waterloo Street. The synagogue, completed in 1878, is the oldest Jewish synagogue in Southeast Asia. Photo: Maghain Aboth Synagogue and Jacob Ballas Centre.

A Jewish wedding at Maghain Aboth Synagogue in the 1980s. Photo: Ronni Pinsler Collection, courtesy of NAS.

Chesed-El Synagogue, which opened in 1905, was commissioned by Sir Manasseh Meyer to give the growing Jewish population in Singapore another house of worship. Photo: Chesed-El Synagogue.

The interior of the Chesed-El Synagogue. Its name means "bountiful mercy and goodness of God" in Hebrew. Photo: Chesed-El Synagogue.

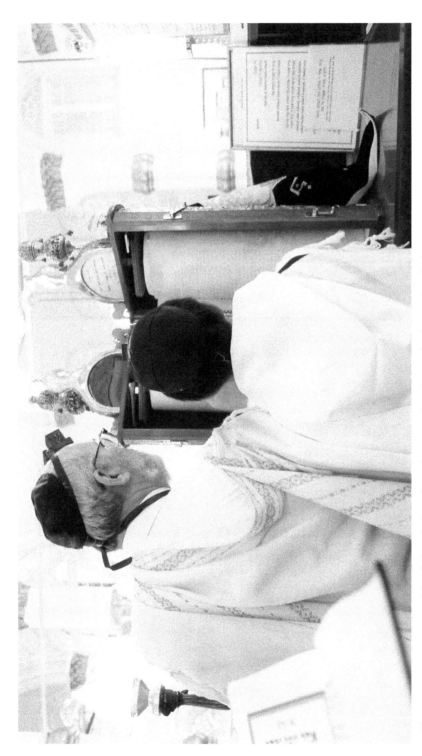

Rabbi Jean Pierre Fettmann, rabbi of Chesed-El, guiding a boy in reading the Torah. Photo: Chesed-El Synagogue.

People's Action Party's Lee Kuan Yew exchanging greetings with Labour Front Party's David Marshall on Polling Day 1955. Led by Lee and Marshall, the two parties fired up and fuelled the local fervour for independence. Photo: Ministry of Information and the Arts Collection, courtesy of NAS.

Singaporean Prime Minister Lee Kuan Yew meeting Israeli President Chaim Herzog during Mr Herzog's official three-day visit to Singapore in 1986. Photo: Saʿar Yaʿacov, courtesy of Israeli Government Press Office.

Singapore's Minister for Education Dr Goh Keng Swee greeting Israeli Foreign Minister Moshe Dayan at a dinner reception hosted by Singapore's Minister for Foreign Affairs S Rajaratnam in Singapore in 1979. Photo: Ministry of Information and the Arts Collection, courtesy of NAS.

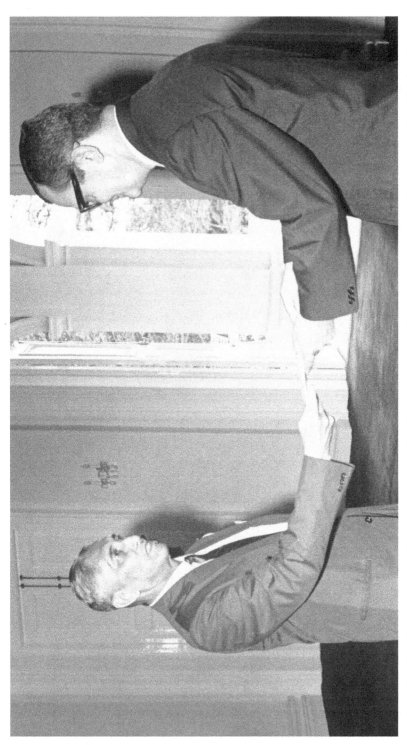

Israeli Ambassador designate Hagay Dikan presenting his credentials to President Yusof Ishak at the Istana on 23 July 1969. Photo: Yusof Ishak Collection, courtesy of NAS.

The AMX-13 tanks made their first public appearance as part of the Singapore Armed Forces mobile column during the National Day Parade at the Padang in 1969. In his chapter, former Foreign Minister George Yeo noted that it was a political decision to do so in front of the Malaysian Prime Minister, who was invited. The late Lee Kuan Yew also wrote in his memoirs that "it had a dramatic effect". Photo: Ministry of Information and the Arts Collection, courtesy of NAS.

Singapore's Senior Minister Lee Kuan Yew meeting Israeli Prime Minister Yitzhak Rabin during Mr Rabin's visit to Singapore in 1993. Photo: Sa'ar Ya'acov, courtesy of Israeli Government Press Office.

Israeli Prime Minister Yitzhak Rabin calls on Prime Minister Goh Chok Tong at the Istana during his visit to Singapore in 1993. Photo: Ministry of Information and the Arts Collection, courtesy of NAS.

Israeli Prime Minister Benjamin Netanyahu with Singaporean Prime Minister Lee Hsien Loong, during his visit to Singapore in February 2017. Photo: Copyright © 2019 Mediacorp Pte Ltd. Image first appeared in www.todayonline.com.

Israeli architect Moshe Safdie checking in on the construction of the Marina Bay Sands integrated resort. Photo: Safdie Architects.

Marina Bay Sands was designed by Mr Moshe Safdie. It has become an iconic symbol of Singapore. Photo: Marina Bay Sands.

Mr Moshe Safdie showing off the model of his design for Jewel, a complex that would unite all of Changi Airport's terminals. Photo: Safdie Architects.

View of Shiseido Forest Valley and HSBC Rain Vortex from the South Viewing Deck at Jewel Changi Airport, designed by Israeli architect Moshe Safdie. Photo: Changi Airport Group.

Mr Dror Feldheim and Mr Joel Bar-El, founders of Trax, the first Israel–Singapore unicorn. Photo: Dror Feldheim and Joel Bar-El.

The Jewish Practice of *Tikkun Olam* and Interfaith Relations in Singapore

Jean Pierre Fettmann

"If you see what needs to be repaired and how to repair it, then you have found a piece of the world that G-d has left for you to complete. But if you only see what is wrong and what is ugly in the world, then it is you yourself that needs repair."

Menachem Mendel Schneerson

In Jewish teachings, we have a concept called *tikkun olam*, which literally means "repairing the world". The origin of this expression goes back to Rabbi Isaac Luria (1534–1572), who was regarded as the father of *Kabbalah*, a term used to describe Jewish mystical activity or school of thought. Luria, who was leader of a community of mystics in Safed, Galilee, in northern Israel during the 16th century, created his own distinctive form of *Kabbalah*. In this form of *Kabbalah*, the Hebrew word *tikkun* first had a spiritual meaning, but in a different context. According to Luria, the idea of *tikkun olam* was based on the notion that during creation, G-d created 10 vessels, which contained the divine "sparks of holiness" or perceptible world of divinity. Sin caused the vessels to shatter, scattering the sparks all over the world and bringing evil into the world. It was the task of Jews to wander and gather the scattered sparks. In *The Biblical Source for Tikkun Olam*, Rabbi Benjamin Blech wrote: "The broken vessels required repair, and this would become the greatest mission of humanity."

The way to restore the divine light to its proper place was through prayer, the study of Torah, and performance of deeds. Thus for Luria, *tikkun* was not synonymous with social justice, as the term is sometimes perceived today; rather, it was a challenge to strive towards perfecting oneself and, as a consequence, the world in which the community was living. Every person's actions have the capacity to affect the cosmos. Unlike earlier medieval mystics who understood the term as improving the spirituality of human beings first, the modern understanding of *tikkun olam* has to do with the idea of changing the world at large. This brings into question whether our quest for universal improvement is better served by concentrating on the individual or on humanity as a whole.

No matter how it is interpreted, *tikkun olam* is a fundamental and important principle of the Jewish life and faith. It is not one of the 613 commandments, but a summary of all of them. This fact readily explains why *tikkun olam* is not found as a *mitzvah* in the Torah. Including it would have diminished its importance, because each individual *mitzvah* is part of a larger set of commandments, each with its own specific claim on our attention and performance.

The concept of *tikkun olam* also raises some important and profound questions. If the world needs to be repaired or fixed, then it seems to imply that what G-d has created is incomplete, that additional effort is required to bring the world to its ultimate state of perfection. In addition, if G-d can create masterpieces, it is not clear how imperfections are permitted. A possible explanation, according to Rabbi Akiva, is that G-d intentionally created humanity to be imperfect, in order to leave room for us to become G-d's partners in creation. Indeed, G-d placed us into an imperfect world and charged us with the responsibility of perfecting it. In this context, the commandments are meant to refine humanity. But this opens up another question: does humanity have the right to interfere in a world created by G-d?

If the world, as it is, expresses G-d's ideal, then any change would be impermissible. Progress would be a sin. Human intervention of any kind would be against the divine will. All human efforts to improve life would thus be a disrespectful affront to the Almighty. But if we look at the story of creation, it ends with the words *asher bara Elohim la'asot* (Genesis 2:3).

Literally, the text means "which G-d created to make". While it is not completely clear to whom the last word, *la'asot*, is addressed, Rabbi Hayim Paltiel (born 1240 CE) suggested that this text teaches that, at a certain point in creation, G-d transferred the responsibility for its completion to humankind, whose specific obligation is to assist G-d in "making" the world. Hence G-d and humankind are partners in creation. As such, it is not only permissible for humanity to continue with the creation, but we are also obliged to change the world for the better. If the world was already perfect, then *tikkun olam* would be meaningless. Not only would it be unnecessary, but it would also be indefensible as an effort to "fix" what G-d had already made, according to the divine will. But if the faults and the flaws of the world are allowed by a G-d who chooses to give humankind the honour of rectifying them, then *tikkun olam* is our obligation.

This concept of *tikkun olam* is revolutionary in the history of religion. It defines faith in dual terms: just as people have faith in G-d, G-d has faith in people. Progress is the purpose of the covenant between the creator and humankind. Hence, our obligation is to use what we have to enhance the lives of others, to fight injustice, to utilise our talents and abilities to serve humanity, and to be creators and not destroyers. Essentially, to ensure that the world is a little bit better when we leave it than it was when we first arrived. This should be the progress.

Such an approach to the world is at the core of Judaism, which lays the foundations for an egalitarian society based not on equality of wealth or power, but on equal access to education, welfare, and human dignity. The prophets never argued that there is injustice, poverty, disease, and violence in the world because that is how G-d wants it to be. Judaism is the call to action and human responsibility with the purpose of making the world better. This is why it is important to live by engaging with the world under a strong moral framework, which Judaism provides. As a result, Jews can be found disproportionately represented in professions such as doctors fighting diseases, lawyers fighting injustice, educators fighting ignorance, economists fighting poverty, entrepreneurs creating helpful technologies, and scientists extending the frontiers of human knowledge.

The Greeks believed in fate and gave the world masterpieces of tragedy. The Jews believe there is no fate that cannot be averted by penitence, prayer, action, and charity. "Judaism is the rejection of tragedy in the name of hope," said Rabbi Lord Jonathan Sacks, chief rabbi of the United Hebrew Congregations of the Commonwealth from 1991 to 2013. Thus *tikkun olam* demands that we do not accept the world as it is, but rather that we view it as what it might become. That remains still an unfinished task. "Yet our glory is to which extent we help to narrow the gap between the world as it is and the world as it might become its potential," said Rabbi Blech.

Besides *tikkun olam*, the concept of interfaith relations also takes centre stage in Jewish theology and moral principles. An example is Shalva National Center, one of Israel's largest centres for disability care and inclusion. Since its inception, the centre has opened new doors of opportunity for people with disabilities and their families. Its state-of-the-art facilities and unique programmes have enhanced the standard of disability services and impacted the lives of people with disabilities in Israel and around the world. Any person, regardless of faith, is accepted. Hence, we see in real life the application of *tikkun olam* and interfaith relations.

Turning to Singapore, we can see how, through the moral and ethical frameworks of *tikkun olam* and interfaith relations provided by their Jewish faith, Jews have helped to play a crucial role in helping the Republic build a society based on peace, harmony and unity. Unlike many places around the world, where hatred against Jews has forced them to migrate or live under fear, Jews in Singapore have been able to pray and live peacefully, following their religion, traditions, and customs. In Singapore, there is a harmony of faiths, where it is understood by everyone that every religion has its own school of teaching and expresses its ideas differently. Singapore has also shown that in order for everyone to be understood and be accepted in a mixed society, exchanges and exploration of traditions are important, as the cornerstone to a peaceful life is to understand the true essence, values, and integrity of various religions.

At the forefront of such efforts in Singapore is the Inter-Religious Organisation (IRO), which was founded back in 1949 exactly with the goal of promoting interfaith dialogue and religious harmony. The Jewish community has been part of the IRO from the very beginning and remains very active today. For example, it arranges exchanges with schools where Jewish people spend some time in Muslim schools and vice versa. The Jewish community also organises regular visits to the synagogues for anyone who is interested in understanding the Jewish faith. Singapore's Prime Minister Lee Hsien Loong once said: "IRO symbolises the ideal of religious harmony. You show that we can transcend our differences. You offer a platform for members of different faiths to learn about one another through interfaith charity projects."

One example was the Tikkun Olam MakeAthon event of making assistive technology for people with disabilities, which took place on 14–16 June 2019. Seventy "makers" (problem solvers, tinkerers, hobbyists, innovators — including engineers, designers, software developers, doctors and occupational therapists) were placed in eight teams and connected with twelve "need-knowers" (individuals with a disability, support workers, family members, etc) who presented their challenges. Teams were tasked with delivering a solution (in the form of a working prototype) by the end of the three-day workshop. All solutions were made available for anyone in the world to access and download from the Tikkun Olam Makers (TOM) web platform. Guests for the closing ceremony of the event included Second Minister for Education Indranee Rajah and then-Israeli Ambassador to Singapore Simona Halperin. During the event, the eight prototypes were presented and the winning teams were announced.

Singapore has been so successful in building and maintaining a harmonious multireligious and multicultural society that Prime Minister Lee Hsien Loong was given the title of 2019 World Statesman, in recognition of his efforts to foster "a society that embraces multiculturalism in which ethnic communities maintain their unique way of life while at the same time living harmoniously". He joins other notable recipients including former French presidents Mr François Hollande (2016) and Mr Nicolas Sarkozy (2008), former British Prime Minister David Cameron (2015), former South Korean President Lee Myung-bak (2009), and German Chancellor Angela Merkel (2007).

This year's award was given in New York City on 23 September 2019 by the Appeal of Conscience Foundation, which was founded by Rabbi Arthur Schneier in 1965. Of the IRO, Rabbi Schneier, the foundation's founder and president, said: "This interfaith coalition of business and religious leaders promotes peace, tolerance and ethnic conflict resolution. The foundation believes that freedom, democracy and human rights are the fundamental values that give nations of the world their best hope for peace, security and shared prosperity." Rabbi Schneier also lauded Mr Lee for "supporting a knowledge-based economy and an education system that provides its citizens with the necessary skills and knowledge to survive in a globally competitive environment and for implementing a renowned world-class health infrastructure".

Judaism has a good basis in the Torah and in modern philosophy to encourage shared learning with our fellow Jews and non-Jews alike. While it may not be our responsibility to educate those who have closed minds, finding a willing ear can help. Ignorance does not always have to be so, and when we have the chance to share knowledge by listening and learning through acts of positive engagement, we might just stop or reverse wilful ignorance. By listening to the concerns of others and starting to build some understanding among ourselves, we can face the future together and build a stronger Singapore.

Jean Pierre Fettmann is rabbi of Singapore's Chesed-El Synagogue.

A Brief History of Jews in Singapore

Victor Sassoon

N ewly founded by the British in 1819, Singapore was intended to be a trading post for both international and regional commerce. Among the earliest to arrive were the Jews, who settled at the mouth of the Singapore River. For them, the entirely new settlement of 19th century Singapore represented a new opportunity and a completely fresh start. Jewish merchants from India and Persia had been actively trading in the region for centuries. However, around 1817, a new wave of Jewish migrants fled to India to escape persecutions by the Ottomans in Persia, joining a local community that had been established earlier.

One of the earliest Singapore records indicated there were only nine Jews in Singapore in 1830.[1] By 1841, the British census of the time showed that the community had grown to 22. A small group of six Jewish men had written to the governing British to request a place for worship and burial. Granted a place near Boat Quay and the Singapore River, without further ado, with neither rabbi nor many families, the small community proceeded to make up the congregation of the first synagogue of Singapore. With this synagogue and burial grounds granted further off as a foothold, the community of Jews in Singapore started to grow as rapidly as the business in the fledgling port. Jewish wives and families were sent for when the living conditions of the

---

[1] Joan Bieder, *The Jews of Singapore* (Singapore: Suntree Media, 2007), p. 21.

port town improved, forming the first clusters of Singapore Jewish homes in the old town area by the river.

The melting pot of Singapore allowed for close interactions between communities, as seen through the account of an East India Company surveyor, John Turnbull Thomson, who was invited to dine with Abraham Solomon, a wealthy merchant and leader of the Jewish community in early Singapore. While this episode seems unremarkable at first glance, one must remember that the two men would never have sat at the same table other than in Singapore at that time. Separated by kosher laws, race and station, the Baghdadi Jewish merchant and the British civil servant would not have had the chance to develop relations, except in Singapore's flexible and small social landscape.

Solomon's house was located within walking distance of the original synagogue by the river. There, Thomson and Solomon ate a kosher, but western-styled meal, accompanied by champagne and coffee. Solomon explained some Jewish practices to his guests, showing Thomson a beautifully written Torah that, in accordance with Jewish law, the British was instructed not to touch. Showing each other cordial intercultural consideration, Thomson was impressed by Solomon's stories of Baghdad as well as his commercial success in Singapore.

Solomon led the community of Jews in Singapore through the 19th century until his death in 1884. During this time, there was both tremendous change as well as growth in the Singapore Jewish community. The rapidly developing economy of early Singapore attracted many people to settle and conduct all sorts of businesses, moving beyond and also out of the original opium and spices trade. Among these were Jewish merchants from India as well as more Baghdadi Jewish migrants. An 1846 census showed that the Jewish community owned six out of then forty-three merchant houses in Singapore. In 1869, the opening of the Suez Canal led to the arrival of more Jews from Europe, adding to the numbers of the Jewish community.

The thriving business of Singapore was attractive to many and, in 1873, a young Baghdadi Jew, Manasseh Meyer, arrived from Calcutta. He would later become the leader of the Jewish community and his commercial success would leave a lasting legacy for generations. By then, the original synagogue by the Singapore River had become too crowded for the growing numbers of Jews. While wealthy Jews moved to other less crowded parts of the town, the majority of migrant Jews formed an enclave around the Sophia Road area. When permission to sell the old synagogue and purchase a plot of land for a new synagogue was sought, Meyer, newly-arrived in Singapore, helped his community to secure approval from the British government. The location of the new synagogue would be at Waterloo Street, within walking distance of the Sophia Road area where many Jews lived so that the Sabbath and holy days could be observed without riding. Maghain Aboth Synagogue at Waterloo Street was completed in 1878 and remains the main Jewish synagogue of Singapore to this day.

Singapore's Jewish community grew and developed apace with the general peace and good fortune of 19th century Singapore. The open business conditions, freedom of religion and multicultural diversity of the island port provided commercial opportunities for an increasingly entrepreneurial population. Some wealthy merchants were able to amass colossal riches, while others were able to secure employment and elevate themselves and their families out of hardship and poverty. Education in English also was progressively available as schools began to open for both boys and girls.

While the Jews of Singapore kept their Sephardi customs and orthodox practices, the middle class of the community began to integrate with the Europeans and British in dress and lifestyle. The influx of Ashkenazi Jews from Western Europe and Russia did not have much impact on the lives of the existing Jewish community who lived in the Sophia Road area. The Ashkenazis' European heritage and connections led them to work with Western firms, hence, their lives did not overlap much with the Jews with Baghdadi roots. However, both the Ashkenazi and Sephardi Jews attended the synagogue and observed the holy days and services together.

By the turn of the century, major Jewish businesses in Singapore had diversified into the new commodities of rubber, tin and textiles. Wealthy

Jewish businessmen also invested in real estate and the stock market. Smaller-sized Jewish businesses prospered by opening shops or general import-export trading. The less affluent orthodox Baghdadi migrant community swelled in the Jewish area, upholding their culture and traditions, while doing small-scale trading in spices and other goods door-to-door, at stalls or in the market. Maghain Aboth Synagogue was filled up with congregation, especially during festivals, as numbers increased. Therefore, Manasseh Meyer, patriarch of the community, planned for the construction of his own place of worship by Belle Vue, his house at Oxley Rise. His Chesed-El Synagogue was open to all upon completion in 1905 and remains in use to this day. While Maghain Aboth Synagogue remained the centre of community worship and activities, everyone was welcomed to join the services at Chesed-El, some distance from the Jewish cluster, with Meyer often hosting activities at Belle Vue. Later on, he also built Talmud Torah Hebrew School at 22B Bencoolen Street, near Maghain Aboth Synagogue, for all Jewish boys to receive teaching in Hebrew and prepare for their *bar mitzvah* when they came of age. After World War Two, girls also benefitted from education in Hebrew at the school.

Even though there were more Jews in Singapore than ever, there were differences in the lives of the rich and poor, whose interactions were limited by status, wealth and lifestyle. The social gap grew wider between the affluent Jewish business families and the poorer immigrant Jews. While the Baghdadi lifestyle was preserved in the Jewish area around Sophia Road, richer and more successful Jews lived further away and emulated the colonial British and Europeans, leading stylish lives while keeping their traditional customs and faith.

Singapore was mostly unaffected by World War One, and business generally continued to thrive with opportunities available for enterprise. The Singapore Jewish community contributed to international Zionist fundraising such as efforts led by the likes of Albert Einstein and Israel Cohen. Even though there were tales of growing antisemitic movements coming out of Europe, it was largely absent in multicultural, multi-ethnic and multifaith Singapore, where all Jews were accepted and wealthy Jews had close to colonial status. A year before his death in 1930, King George V knighted Manasseh Meyer, the patriarch of Singapore Jews, for his public service and good works.

The 1930s Great Depression had an impact on the price of tin and rubber in Singapore. Nevertheless, as many Jewish businesses had diversified into other areas and real estate, its economic impact on the community was largely neutral. In 1934, then a young man in his 20s, David Marshall, Singapore's first Chief Minister, started a magazine for Singapore Jews with some of his young friends. Even though the publication ceased in 1937, it heralded the beginning of his community activities and leadership in the future. During this time, Marshall became the first Jewish man from Singapore to complete his legal studies and be called to the bar in London. He returned in 1937 to become a criminal trial lawyer.

However, the world was about to change with the outbreak of World War Two. Migrant Jews from Europe began to arrive in Singapore, bringing numbers up to some 2,000. While war broke out in Europe, the Pacific War engulfed most of Asia and consumed Singapore too. On 7 December 1941, without warning, in the middle of the night, bombs started to fall as air raids by the Japanese started the Pacific War. As the Japanese occupied Malaya and drew closer to Singapore, many of the Singapore Jewish community evacuated the island in haste. Many women and children who had connections with Indian Jews, especially in Bombay, fled on ships to India. The Japanese stormed into Singapore from Malaya and the unprepared British surrendered on 15 February 1942. Thus began the Japanese Occupation of Singapore.

From a population of some 1,500 Jews who lived in pre-Occupation Singapore, there were only approximately 600 to 700 remaining when the Japanese took over the island. The much diminished community watched in horror as the Japanese culled the Chinese in a massacre of unknown thousands. Between 5,000 and 25,000 Chinese men in Singapore were rounded up and machine-gunned to death. Random disappearances, beheading, whipping, executions, abduction and torture were used to freeze any resistance to the Japanese. Initially treated as neutral, the Singapore Jews were ordered to register themselves at Orchard Road Police Station after a month of the Occupation. There, they received white armbands with a red stripe bearing their names, registration numbers, and the Japanese word *Uta* which means Jew.[2]

Food ran scarce and a black market of goods started to thrive, with the Japanese "banana money" replacing the Singapore currency. While industry and business dried up, some Jews were able to sell their jewellery, watches, paintings and other goods to get by; others were not so fortunate. Local people were reduced to selling tea or spices in the market. Tapioca and other vegetables were planted for food as rice and other food were rationed since Singapore had imported almost all its foodstuff. Information was controlled by the Japanese, who were punitive without tolerance. More than ever, the Jews gathered around Maghain Aboth Synagogue for prayer, community, and exchange of news, and collections were made to help the poorest. Despite their alliance with Adolf Hitler and the Nazis, the Japanese initially treated the Jews with respect and undertook not to interfere with the practice of their Jewish faith.

But that lasted only a year. On 5 April 1943, about a hundred Jewish men were suddenly rounded up and interned at Changi jail. This exercise was purportedly the result of some Jews making a gesture at the officers of a German ship that had arrived in Singapore.[3] The rest of the 500- to 600-strong community remained free. The interned men were still able to observe prayers and holy days within the camp where they occupied a section. Food was just sufficient at first and the overcrowded conditions were improved somewhat by the ingenuity of the earlier internees. The situation changed after 10 October 1943, when the Japanese clamped down on the Changi internee camp on suspicion of radio intelligence being broadcast from within. Food rations were cut to starvation level and from then on

---

[2] Bieder, *The Jews*, p. 98.
[3] Ibid., p. 101.

all went hungry. By the last months of the Occupation, the internees were dying of malnutrition.

The Jewish men, women and children left outside had to make do with ever harder conditions in Singapore as supplies of everything, from medicines to food, also began to run out. On 1 May 1944, the Japanese moved civilian prisoners, including the interned Jewish men, from the camp in Changi prison to a camp at Sime Road at the former Royal Air Force headquarters. There, they were allowed to have family visits for half an hour on Sundays. Allied air raids began to strike Singapore in November 1944, raising hopes of rescue as well as fears of reprisals on the population from the Japanese. Then, late in 1944, the Jewish internees were told to build six new huts that could accommodate one hundred each for themselves and other internees. The rest of the Jewish community were ordered to report to the Sime Road camp on 25 March 1944. They would spend the last six months of the war there.

On 12 September 1944, the Japanese surrendered. The Jewish internees, however, remained at the camp for a few more weeks, for, even though the British military had returned to Singapore, the town was devastated and they had nowhere to go. The times were chaotic and hard but the Torah scrolls were unscathed and the synagogues were returned to the community. Before the return of the Singapore Jewish community leaders, the Jews organised themselves, with Fred Isaacs, EB Solomon and EM Sharbanee taking their place to see to the poor, recoup community finances, and manage the synagogues. In 1946, David Marshall returned as a hero to Singapore after recovering from hard labour in Hokkaido, where he was interned alongside the colonial Allied forces during the war. Forbidden to enlist to participate in the war effort, he and Charles Simon had joined the Singapore Volunteer Corps, a Straits Settlements volunteer force formed by the British. Simon had been transported to work on the infamous Thai-Burma Death Railway, while Marshall was sent to Hokkaido. Against huge odds, they endured horrific conditions and survived the war. Soon after, the Jewish Welfare Association (now the Jewish Welfare Board) was established on 27 June 1946 at a meeting chaired by Marshall.

The mission of the new association was to care for Jewish community welfare as well as religious, educational, charitable and cultural activities. It played a vital role in the Singapore Jewish community. Over the next few years, the association helped the poor survive and also assisted those wishing to emigrate and make a fresh start. The war had interrupted the education of the young and, without a rabbi, the international Habonim youth movement took root in post-war Singapore to cheer and encourage some 80 younger community members with religious, educational and scouting activities. For some who had only heard about Palestine, the first time they learnt about the state of Israel was through their Habonim activities and their imagination was captured by the possibility of living in the new Jewish state.

Over 100 Jews in Singapore made *Aliyah* to Israel after the war. The community numbers dwindled, but the arrival of Rabbi Jacob Shababo from Egypt in 1949 gave spiritual leadership to those who stayed in Singapore. The young people started their own Menorah Club that served to organise fun, social activities for them as well as the rest of the community. Talmud Torah school also resumed classes in the 1950s against a backdrop of political changes that were about to change the destiny of Singapore.

Besides taking charge of the Jewish Welfare Association from 1946 to 1952, David Marshall also pursued a brilliant legal career and entered political life. In 1947, he helped form the Progressive Party, a conservative group that was aligned with British interests. Disgruntled by the British, he left the party by 1952 to lead the Labour Front Party, a coalition of Labour splinter groups. Leading with his eloquence, neutrality and wits, Marshall was able to bring various factions together in unity against British rule. The end of an era of Singapore as a colony approached with local elections in April 1955.

With his outspoken criticism of British rule, Marshall struck a chord with ordinary voters who were tired of colonialism. The Labour Front won the elections with a majority, with Lee Kuan Yew's People's Action Party coming in second. Thus, Marshall, a Singapore Jew, became the first elected Chief Minister of Singapore. Between David Marshall and Lee Kuan Yew, their parties fuelled a local fervour for independence, based on resentment of colonial imperialism and racial discrimination. After pushing for total self-government, Marshall stepped down from office in April 1956 after the British refused Singapore the veto over its defence. While Marshall gave voice to the wishes of the people of Singapore for self-determination, it was Lee and his People's Action Party that forged a unified, multilingual, multiracial Singapore which would fulfil many of the ideas that they had originally incubated.

As Singapore's economy began to boom once more in the post-war years, the Jewish community in Singapore slowly began to grow, too, with returning Jews as well as the arrival of expatriate Jews from the West. While the original Singapore Baghdadi community did not ever fully regroup after the war, newer members of the community joined. The Jews in Singapore came to prominence in finance, law, medicine and business as well as specialist fields in fashion and jewellery, among others. Jacob Ballas was one such example of an individual whose rags-to-riches journey propelled him to the chair of the Singapore Stock Exchange. The contributions of the Jews in Singapore to the development of the island-nation have been disproportionally huge compared to their small numbers in relation to the rest of the Singapore population.

Recognition for the Jews by the government of Singapore came after David Marshall's death in 1995. Maghain Aboth and Chesed-El synagogues were recognised as national monuments in 1997 and 1998 respectively for their spiritual and architectural value. A public exhibition of the Jews in Singapore was held at the former Singapore History Museum for six months in 1999. The community celebrated the 125th anniversary of Maghain Aboth Synagogue in 2004 with Singapore's President SR Nathan, diplomatic dignitaries, Singapore's Inter-Religious Organisation, and rabbis from around the world.

Since 2007, the community now also meets for activities at Jacob Ballas Centre built by the Jacob Ballas Estate next to Maghain Aboth Synagogue. The Jews in Singapore are an accepted part of the diverse community of

Singapore and remain distinct for keeping the Jewish faith, traditional customs, and family values. As blessings are always said in the synagogue for the Republic of Singapore, the State of Israel, and the congregation, the Jews of Singapore continue to go about their busy lives in peace to this day.

Bibliography

Bieder, Joan. *The Jews of Singapore*. Singapore: Suntree Media, 2007.

Goldstein, Jonathan. *Jewish Identities in East and Southeast Asia*. Berlin: De Gruyter, 2015.

Nathan, Eze. *The History of Jews in Singapore, 1830–1945*. Singapore: Herbilu Editorial & Marketing Services, 1986.

Victor Sassoon is executive chairman of Sassoon Investment Corporation. He is also president of the Jewish Welfare Board and trustee of the Jewish Charity Trust and the Jacob Ballas Trust.

The History of Jewish Synagogues in Singapore

Edmund Lim

The history of Jewish synagogues in Singapore is closely intertwined with the history of the Jewish community. In the various places where the Jews have settled, they would want to build synagogues, their houses of worship. This was also the case in Singapore. For many in the Jewish community, the synagogue was a place to pray, worship, study the Torah, and meet their brethren.

The first official record of Jews in Singapore can be found in an 1830 census. The records indicated that there were "nine traders of Jewish faith". Singapore was founded in 1819 by Thomas Stamford Raffles, before becoming a free port in 1822, attracting more and more traders from different parts of the world. Among those who came were Jewish traders from the Middle East and India, then a British colony.

Another official record indicated that, by 1841, there was a Jewish community of eighteen males and four females. Though this group was small, they wanted to set up a synagogue and fulfil their religious duties. Ezra Ezekiel, Joseph Dwek Cohen and Nassim Joseph Ezra discussed their proposal with the British authorities and received a government lease on a small plot of land to establish a synagogue along a street in the heart of the business district. This street was subsequently named Synagogue Street.

The First Synagogue in Singapore

This very first synagogue in Singapore was located in a row of shophouses. Conveniently located near Boat Quay, it looked like any other shophouse. It was used primarily during Sabbath and on days of religious festivals when the community was able to gather a *minyan* or quorum of 10 men. This land was rented at a nominal rate. The lease had a proviso that stated its validity as long as the site was for "divine worship". Eventually, after World War Two, this two-storey shophouse was demolished.

By 1846, the census revealed that the Jewish community in Singapore was growing in size and wealth. For instance, six of the forty-three merchant houses on this island were Jewish-owned. Many of the Jews were of Sephardic origins.

A letter dated 24 December 1854 described this first synagogue in Singapore and the community. Benjamin Cook wrote to his friend Harry Russell stating:

> We have a small number here … they have a synagogue in the Chinese town, just a shophouse that they use, and it is here that you may see their patriarch Abraham Solomon, who not only leads their community in this promised land, but indeed looks exactly I am sure as Moses looked — tall with long flowing robes, a turban and a great white beard.

Jacob Sapphier, a Jewish traveller, noted in 1858 that there were "some 20 families of our brethren" in this "city with a beautiful harbour where many ships anchored". He also observed that the Jewish people in Singapore were dressed in the Middle Eastern traditional style, with the women in gowns or long loose dresses (*moomoos*) with long sleeves and lace collars, and the men in long buttoned vests with topcoats and turbans (*fezes*).

The Jewish population continued to grow. From 1871 to 1874, census records indicated that there were about 57 Jews in Singapore. That first synagogue was no longer able to comfortably accommodate the growing community.

Furthermore, the Jews started living further away from the central business district and moved into the residential areas around Dhoby Ghaut, Adis Road, Prinsep Street, Selegie Road, Waterloo Street and Sophia Road. There was a need for a new synagogue. By the late 1870s, there were close to 200 Jews in Singapore.

Maghain Aboth Synagogue

In 1873, Manasseh Meyer, a trustee of the first synagogue, sought permission from British Attorney General Thomas Braddell to construct a new synagogue. Meyer was a very rich, successful and influential trader. The British approved the request and the Jewish community was allocated a site to build this new synagogue, along Church Street, which is currently known as Waterloo Street.

On 4 April 1878, the new synagogue named Maghain Aboth, which meant "shield of our fathers" in Hebrew, was consecrated. This specially designed synagogue had an entrance arch that was sufficiently large for a horse-drawn carriage to pass through. With its main entrance facing Jerusalem, this synagogue also had large windows and a high ceiling to make it a little cooler in this hot and humid tropical climate.

In addition, there was a *mikvah* or bath area for Jewish women to use for ritual purification. At first, this single-storey synagogue had no separate space for women. Subsequently, Meyer, the Sephardic leader of the Jewish community in colonial Singapore, sponsored the construction of a wooden gallery in the synagogue for ladies so that they could be included in the religious activities.

Maghain Aboth became the religious centre and the thriving hub for the Jewish community. Jewish families chose to live near this synagogue in order to conveniently attend daily prayers and the weekly Shabbat services. In 1998, Maghain Aboth became a national monument and remains in use by the Jewish community.

Chesed-El Synagogue

As Singapore grew, its population, including the Jewish community, expanded. Census records revealed that the Jewish population increased from about 200 in the late 1870s to almost 500 by 1902. Maghain Aboth Synagogue became packed with people, particularly during religious festivals.

Then Meyer, a philanthropist and business tycoon, decided to build a new synagogue which could comfortably accommodate 300 people on his Oxley Rise property. It was to be designed by Regent Alfred John Bidwell from Swan & McLaren, then the biggest architectural company in Singapore.

In 1905, this spacious and lovely synagogue named Chesed-El, which meant "bountiful mercy and goodness of God" in Hebrew, opened for service.

On Friday morning of 14 April 1905, Meyer led his people in prayers, Torah readings and thanksgiving as part of the synagogue dedication service. The detailed text used during this event can be found in the book, *Rav Pe'alim*, written by Rabbi Yosef Chayim in Hebrew.

Meyer would go to Chesed-El Synagogue daily for the morning and evening services, continuing to do so, well into his 80s. In his old age, he would wear a horn-shaped hearing aid and listen attentively to the services.

For the daily prayers in the synagogue, Meyer would pay for the "*minyan* men" so that there would be a quorum of 10 men in attendance in order for the services to be held. In this way, the daily religious services could be conducted consistently.

Besides contributing to the building and maintenance of the two synagogues in Singapore, Maghain Aboth and Chesed-El, Meyer set up a Hebrew school or "Talmud Torah", which provided the children of the community with basic Jewish education. Furthermore, he funded the salaries of the teachers and the meals of the children in this school.

In November 1922, Albert Einstein visited Singapore to raise funds to set up the Hebrew University in Jerusalem. In Einstein's words, Chesed-El was a "magnificent synagogue, which was actually built for the purpose of communication between Croesus and Jehovah". Croesus was an extremely rich sixth century king and Einstein regarded Meyer as "Croesus". Einstein also described Meyer's home, Belle Vue at Oxley Drive, as "a palace, with Moorish charming halls, located on the top of a hill with a view of the city and sea".

Einstein recalled Meyer's appearance in detail: "Croesus is still a slender, upright 80-year-old man with a strong will; a small grey-pointed beard, a thin reddish face, a narrow Jewish bent nose, clever, somewhat shrewd eyes, a small black cap on a well-arched forehead."

Meyer donated generously to educational causes such as the Hebrew University of Jerusalem. He also built a synagogue in Jerusalem. In Singapore, he donated to various causes, including Saint Joseph's Institution, his alma mater. He also contributed what was then a huge sum of S$150,000 to Raffles College, which subsequently became the National University of Singapore (NUS). To recognise Meyer as one of the top donors, the college named one of the major buildings on the campus after him. Today, the Manasseh Meyer Building in NUS's Bukit Timah campus is gazetted as a national monument in memory of this outstanding leader of the Jewish community.

For his many contributions in Singapore and overseas, Meyer was knighted by the British in 1929. *The Straits Times* stated on 1 March 1929 that he was "a leader of an influential community in the Colony" as well as "a man of great wealth who ... contributed lavishly to various local and imperial causes, in addition to having done a vast amount of good in Malaya".

Manasseh Meyer lived to a ripe old age of 87 and passed away on 1 July 1930. Chesed-El Synagogue was the venue of his morning funeral service. Even in his final will, he never forgot the Jewish community and synagogue. He willed that "my Synagogue in Oxley Rise and my Hebrew School in Bencoolen Street ... be upkept and maintained substantially as [during] my lifetime, including food for the pupils and salaries for teachers out of my estate". Furthermore, Meyer wanted the "residue of the net income" of his funds to be allocated "for charitable purposes for the benefit of persons of the Jewish religion or in support of charitable organisations or educational establishments for the benefit of persons of Jewish religion".

For the past 89 years, the funds from his estate have continued to benefit Maghain Aboth and Chesed-El, as well as the Jewish Welfare Board (JWB) and the Hebrew School. The JWB has helped to care for the needy and the Jewish community.

Talmud Torah Hebrew School

Built by Meyer at the start of the 20th century, the Talmud Torah Hebrew School at Bencoolen Street provided a Jewish education for the boys in the community. They would learn Hebrew and the reading of the Torah. They would also be prepared for their *bar mitzvah*, which is an important religious milestone when they would be called to read the Torah in the synagogue at the age of 13.

In addition to a Jewish education, the boys were provided with meals. After World War Two, the school opened to Jewish girls too. Generations of Jewish children benefited from their Jewish education at the Hebrew School, which continues till this day.

Hubs for the Jewish Community

Along with the Talmud Torah Hebrew School, the two synagogues in Singapore were hubs for the Jewish community. Many of the Jewish community in Singapore were Sephardic Jews. A good number descended from Iraqi Jewish migrants and many were Orthodox Jews. There were also a smaller number of fairer Ashkenazi Jews who came from Europe.

The synagogues were open to residents and visitors. One of the prominent overseas visitors was British-born Israel Cohen, who promoted the restoration of the Jewish homeland. After meeting the Jewish communities in Australia, China, Hong Kong, Japan and the Philippines, Cohen arrived in Singapore in February 1921.

Cohen wanted to inform the various Jewish communities about England's Balfour Declaration, which supported the establishment of a Jewish homeland in Palestine. In addition, Cohen wanted to raise donations and resources to support this goal. His biggest donor was Manasseh Meyer, who gave him a substantial sum of 3,000 pounds. Furthermore, Meyer supported Cohen in setting up a Zionist Society on this island of Singapore.

Another notable visitor was the Japanese Minister for Foreign Affairs who visited Maghain Aboth in 1942, during the Japanese Occupation of Singapore. He assured the Jewish community that their religious practices would not face any Japanese interference.

Japanese Occupation

During the first year of the difficult Occupation period, the Jewish community gathered at the synagogue to pray, meet, socialise, comfort, and help one other. They supported the poorer ones in the community and sought solace in Judaism.

The situation changed in April 1943. About 3,500 Jews were relocated and interned in Changi camp. Approximately 550 Jews were left in the city of Singapore. This smaller community could still gather at Maghain Aboth Synagogue for prayers and fellowship.

In May 1944, the Jewish interns were relocated from Changi camp to Sime Road camp. Life was tough during the Japanese Occupation. Food and medicine were inadequate.

During the Japanese Occupation from February 1942 to September 1945, the two synagogues were not badly damaged. During the latter part of the Occupation, Maghain Aboth Synagogue was used by the Japanese to store iron and ammunition. Though the cane benches went missing, the sacred Torah scrolls were not damaged or discarded. The Japanese used Chesed-El Synagogue as a Buddhist temple so the facilities and venue were treated with respect.

The Japanese surrendered in August 1945. After World War Two ended, the British returned to Singapore. The Jewish interns were allowed passage on ships to British India, Australia and England to meet with their extended family members overseas. This led to a significant decline in the size of the Jewish community in Singapore.

The Restoration

After the Japanese Occupation ended, 27 Jewish community members in Singapore gathered at Maghain Aboth Synagogue in October 1945 to discuss their plans to take care of the community and the synagogues. Members such as Fred Isaacs, EB Solomon and EM Sharbanee worked to restore the synagogues and the well-being of the community.

On 27 June 1946, a group of Jewish members formed the Jewish Welfare Board (JWB) to look into the welfare of the community and its needy members. The first president of the JWB was David Marshall, who later became Singapore's first Chief Minister. In the post-war era, the JWB played a leading role in taking care of the synagogues as well as the community.

After the formation of the State of Israel in 1948, certain Jewish people in Singapore wanted to migrate to Israel (*Aliyah*). The JWB assisted a number of them in their migration, despite its limited resources.

In 1953, the Jewish youth in the community formed the Menorah Club to provide recreational, social, spiritual and cultural activities. They met at the Talmud Torah on Shabbat afternoons. They told stories, sang, danced and organised a range of events, including debates, lectures, movie screenings, concerts and outings.

To support the preschool children in the community, the Jewish preschool was established in January 1955, with the support of the JWB and the Sir Manasseh Meyer Talmud Torah Trust. The Talmud Torah continued to provide a Jewish education for the community with about 40 students.

In 1955, there were approximately 700 Jews in Singapore. A substantial number migrated to countries such as Israel, Australia, England and the United States of America. By 1978, the community decreased to about 450 members and by about 1985 there were only about 250 Singaporean members left. Though the community was small, the members contributed actively in the political, legal and economic spheres.

Progressing On

In 1978, the community celebrated the 100th anniversary of Maghain Aboth Synagogue. It was a milestone in the history of the community. Ms Felice Isaacs, then-president of the JWB, noted: "We can take full pride for the part we have played in the successful transition which Singapore had made to full statehood." This celebration in multiracial and multireligious Singapore included a Christian bishop, Buddhist monks and a Sikh priest, as well as then-Israeli Ambassador Itzhak Navon and Jews from various countries.

In the 1990s, business leader and philanthropist Jacob Ballas served as JWB president. The JWB hired Rabbi Modechai Abergel, a Sephardic Orthodox rabbi. Together with Rabbi Abergel, the Jewish community leaders contributed to the revival of Jewish life in Singapore.

In addition to the services in the Sephardic Orthodox synagogues of Maghain Aboth and Chesed-El, starting from 1991, the Jewish expatriate community in Singapore had their own services in private homes. This community formed the United Hebrew Congregation (UHC). Many were Ashkenazi Jews from the West. The UHC would subsequently have its services at the American Club. Some UHC members would attend services at the local synagogues too.

Along with the local Jewish families, some of the Jewish expatriate families sent their toddlers to Ganenu Jewish Learning Centre, set up in the mid-1990s by Mrs Simcha Abergel, the rabbi's wife. Similarly, the Talmud Torah was also open to the children of the expatriate Jewish community. Over the past three decades, the expatriate Jewish members also formed part of the Jewish community in Singapore.

In November 2004, Maghain Aboth celebrated its 125th anniversary and the guests included SR Nathan, then-President of Singapore, ambassadors from Israel and the United States, along with Singaporeans and Jewish friends from various countries. From a one-storey building, Maghain

Aboth Synagogue has become a thriving hub for the Jewish community. Frank Benjamin, then-JWB president, said that the "community leaders are encouraged by the prospects of a flourishing Jewish future in Singapore".

The 100th anniversary of Chesed-El Synagogue was celebrated in 2005. In addition to the late President Nathan, Mr George Yeo, then-Foreign Minister of Singapore, and Singapore's former Ambassador-at-Large Tommy Koh, various prominent leaders and Jewish community members took part in the memorable celebrations.

Both the synagogues, which today are national monuments in Singapore, have been beautifully renovated and restored. They continue to serve as important places of prayer for the Jewish community. The Jacob Ballas Estate funded the construction of the seven-storey Jacob Ballas Centre next to Maghain Aboth Synagogue. Officially inaugurated in November 2007, this centre contains an auditorium, library, meeting rooms, *mikvah* for Jewish ladies, dining facilities, offices for JWB staff and Rabbi Abergel, as well as accommodation for the rabbi, his family and guests.

In 2019, the construction of a new three-storey building adjacent to Chesed-El Synagogue was completed. On the ground floor is a communal hall, which holds 220 for a seated dinner, as well as a state-of-the-art kosher, meat and dairy kitchen. The second floor will serve as a nursery and preschool for Jewish children. The top floor is an open-air outdoor dining area, which will also be used as a *succah*, or temporary hut, during the Feast of Succoth. This Reuben Meyer Centre is named after Manasseh Meyer's son, who had always supported his father's vision of helping the Jewish community, and was sponsored by the trustees of the Reuben Meyer Trust, including Ms Felice Isaacs and Dr Stanley Isaacs.

The Maghain Aboth and Chesed-El synagogues, along with the Jacob Ballas Centre and Reuben Meyer Centre, continue to thrive as vital hubs for the small and successful Jewish community. The synagogues also form a key part of multiracial, multireligious Singapore, which promotes religious harmony and respect among people of various faiths.

Edmund Lim is currently a senior vice-president in the education sector. He co-wrote a book on Chesed-El Synagogue and has also written a biography of Jacob Ballas, an outstanding Jewish philanthropist and leader.

The Story of Israeli Architecture in Singapore

Moshe Safdie

My first visit to Singapore was originally planned for October 1973. Singapore was then eight years old, and I was invited by Israel's attaché, Brigadier-General Ephrain Poran, who suggested I meet with the Minister for National Development. Singapore, he said, had planned a major housing programme for its population, and the minister might be interested in the experimental modular housing concepts we had evolved for Habitat 67 six years earlier. This trip did not to come to pass; it was interrupted by the Six Day War.

In 1976, Mr Robin Low, a Singaporean businessman, shipbuilder and real estate developer, visited my office in Montreal, Canada. He had heard about the prefabrication methods of Habitat and thought, given the slump in the shipping business, to divert his shipyard in Singapore to producing residential modules. I flew with him to Singapore for my first visit. Two sites were identified — one downtown at the head of Orchard Road in Ardmore and the other in Tampines, not far from the Changi Airport. With great excitement, we embarked on developing proposals for both. The Tampines site would be built with prefabricated modules, a sprawling site accommodating some thousands of units. It would be an opportunity to apply industrial housing techniques to middle-income housing.

The Ardmore site evolved into two luxury residential towers. The towers were realised in 1985 and were very successful real estate ventures, until 2006, when they were demolished to make way for two much taller towers, enabled by the changed zoning for the site. In the 1980s, I returned to Singapore many times. We were commissioned to design a project for Crane Hill Road, triplet towers interconnected into a singular complex, now known as The Edge on Cairnhill. My involvement with Singapore expanded over the years. I was invited by the Housing and Development Board (HDB) to develop an alternative plan for Simpang New Town. The mandate was to develop new concepts and new ideas that the HDB might consider beyond their practice at the time. At that time, I was based in Harvard, so I would involve some of my Singaporean students in the exercise, working out of my Boston office. Our innovation was to propose diverse typologies, unlike the single typology complexes of the HDB. Low-, mid- and high-rise typologies would be combined to achieve an environment which would feel less dense than a single typology complex. When the model arrived in Singapore, there was doubt that our proposal offered the same density as the HDB scheme. The plans were carefully measured to confirm indeed that what appeared to be a lesser density had met the requirements of HDB development. As it turned out, the concept was too much of a divergence from HDB's practices at that time and it was not realised.

Several years later, I participated as a member of the jury for the international architectural design competition for the Duxton Hill HDB housing complex to be built in downtown Singapore. The competition was established to explore new housing concepts. Indeed, the first, second and third choices were all innovative, each in their own way. I served on the jury with several Singaporean colleagues, as well as with Mr Fumihiko Maki, the eminent Japanese architect. The now completed Pinnacle@Duxton project ushered the HDB into a new era of more adventurous and experimental designs.

Over the years, I became aware of the many forms of co-operation and collaboration between Singapore and Israel. It always occurred to me how both Israel and Singapore emerged out of British systems: Singapore as a colony in 1965, and Israel as a British mandate in 1948. Both inherited the British bureaucracy and its civil administration systems. As an Israeli, I often envied Singapore's innovation in adapting the British system to its own need. Certainly in the area of my own discipline — city planning, urban design and architecture — Singapore has led the world in embracing a policy of affirmative intervention of individual developments towards achieving a more cohesive and workable city. Similarly, its innovations in traffic control, and its years-ahead approach to providing infrastructure, as it was anticipated rather than after the fact, leave Israelis envious, and, I would even say, in awe.

In 2007, we were invited by Las Vegas Sands (LVS) Chairman Sheldon Adelson to join LVS in preparing a proposal for the Marina Bay Sands integrated resort project. This was an international competition, drawing some of the greatest talents in development and architecture worldwide. Impressively, the government did not ask the developers to compete on the price of the land. Rather, it fixed the land cost and stated that the winning project would be selected based on the quality of programme and design — meaning, the project that makes the greatest contribution to Singapore would be selected.

We were delighted to learn, five months later, that LVS, together with us and our design, had been selected by the government. It seemed that many years of working in Singapore, and our intimate knowledge of the country and the objectives of its administration contributed to our ability to come up with a scheme that resonated with the government's objectives. None of us was aware at the time that Marina Bay Sands would become an iconic symbol of Singapore. While we were all aware that many of the design elements would be architecturally spectacular, the magic that etches a building in the public psyche is something you can hope for but not anticipate.

When we joined hands with CapitaLand to submit a proposal to Changi Airport for a new centre that would unify all the Changi terminals, we wondered how we would come up with an encore, a complex that would, once again, ignite the public psyche and resonate with Singapore's dreams and aspirations.

The Jewel, as it has come to be known, was conceived to provide a programmatic list of retail and airport facilities, together with "an attraction". This attraction should be one that would appeal to residents of Singapore as well as travellers, but what form it was to take was yet to be determined. Knowing the commitment of Singapore as a Garden City, or a City in a Garden as Singapore's founding father Lee Kuan Yew had put it, that vision could be celebrated by creating a magical garden, one filled with various attractions for the young and old, but which, at the same time, could be an uplifting place of calmness and serenity.

Once again, our proposal was selected and CapitaLand entered into a joint venture with Changi Airport. Jewel held its initial opening in June 2019. The hundreds of thousands who visited it during its first week of opening demonstrated the enthusiasm and excitement Singaporeans manifested towards this new complex. The Valley Garden, with its waterfall nourished by the Republic's abundant rainfall, has become yet another iconic symbol of Singapore.

In recent decades, we continued working with CapitaLand on many projects in Singapore and in China. As such, in the many years of my interaction with Singaporeans in the business community, as well as public officials, I always found that my Israeli roots opened doors. Many were familiar with Israel; they had visited either during military service or under other assignments. Many now travel there as tourists. As for Israelis, Singapore has become a destination, and I would even say is regarded by many as a country to be envied for its extraordinary achievements, given its similarity in scale and size to Israel. Israel's emphases on education and the development of high-tech industries resonate with Singapore's ambitions. Many co-operative efforts are now underway.

We have enjoyed having an office in Singapore for the past 15 years. While I personally hold Israeli, as well as Canadian and United States citizenships, I often feel that I have a fourth one in Singapore. That is certainly true in terms of engagement and a feeling of belonging to this city-state where I have spent so much time in the past 40 years.

Moshe Safdie is an architect, urban planner, educator, theorist and author. A citizen of Israel, Canada and the United States, Mr Safdie designed two Singaporean icons — Marina Bay Sands and Jewel Changi Airport.

My Childhood in Singapore (1966–1969)

Raanan Boral

In the summer of 1966, just after I turned nine years old, my father, older brother and I landed in Singapore, less than a year after the expulsion of Singapore from the Malaysian Federation. Singapore was an independent state.

My father served as a United Nations economics consultant, and decided to take up a position in Singapore. I was in third grade and my brother, Haran (in the Bible, Haran was Abraham's brother), was in eighth grade. Upon landing, we were registered at the Singapore American School, which for us was revolutionary compared to what we had known at home. Classes were small; we wore blue pants and white shirts with the school emblem. The school was huge, with large sports fields and a nice cafeteria with sweet chocolate milk.

We had a maid living with us, an old Chinese woman named Abin, who, and I apologise that I remember her for only one thing, made terrible food. We had a driver, Mohamed, who hardly said a word and drove us quietly to school every morning. For a nine-year-old coming from a young Israel, Singapore appeared high class and modern. But only in part as I learned quickly, as at that time Singapore was quite far from being modern and possessing the associated economic class that came with it.

The other side of Singapore that I came to know was dirtier, with an inconvenient odour. The smell came from the canals or ducts along the roadsides to drain the rainwater, and, as we later learned, to partly drain sewage as well. We liked and disliked those channels. The small, narrow and deep ones "swallowed" our baseballs and tennis balls, unless someone shoved his hand quickly into the "water" to extract the ball. But we swam in the wide and deep ones to catch catfish and guppies. We would release the catfish immediately after receiving the appropriate recognition for the mere catch and more so for the size of the fish. But the catching of guppies developed into a thriving market of guppy exchange among us, the children of the 8 Napier Road compound. The males guppies grew relatively large with colourful tails, thus creating "value" and developing what, in those days, must surely have been one of the largest commercial activities in the young state of Singapore.

We lived at 8D Napier Road (D representing the fourth out of the four buildings in the compound), just across the fence from Gleneagles Hospital, which in those days was of course much smaller than what it is today. It constituted only the old colonial building, which I am not sure still exists today, and a wide, well-kept garden. 8 Napier Road was a compound of four buildings, with parking lots in between that served as playgrounds in the afternoons and weekends, and as a great field to launch fireworks during Chinese New Year.

Chinese New Year was our most special event of the year, much more than our own Jewish holidays, and for a good reason. We would save a huge sum of money during the year so that we could buy large quantities of fireworks for the celebration. Huge, not just large, quantities. It was a sight to be seen, that words cannot describe. We had no doubt that we were the best on the island during Chinese New Year, as we were sure we lit up the sky more than anyone else. The neighbours, especially those with no children, were less enthusiastic about this activity as their porches received a significant quantity of the rockets that we fired. I remember this day as a worthy reward for a year's savings.

When the parked cars left us no room to play, we would cross the fence to Gleneagles Hospital and its wonderful garden. When there were too many of us, we would be chased away from the garden. But when it was only my brother and me, we used two palm trees as a goalpost so that my brother could train me in football. Many years later, my brother volunteered as a coach for several years in the Little League in Austin, Texas. I have no doubt that his experience in Gleneagles Hospital contributed to this part of his voluntary career.

When the parking lots were full and we couldn't play on the hospital grass, we moved to the next stop — the Singapore Botanic Gardens just a few minutes' walk from home. Thus, occasionally, the Botanic Gardens were our de facto backyard. We played hide-and-seek, hands up, and other games that the bushes accommodated. If the parking lots had their shortcomings — parked cars — and the hospital had its shortcoming — someone ordering us to leave — the Gardens had theirs as well — the baboons. We learned to avoid them, but, from time to time, the games had to stop when one of us was attacked by a bunch of monkeys. In some cases, the result was bloody and painful.

If I were asked to summarise my childhood in Singapore of the late 1960s in one word, *freedom* would be the word I would use to describe my personal feelings and experiences as a young child. For example, during the addition of a lane to Napier Road, we, the children of the compound, joined the workers in shovelling and moving earth. In return, at the end of the day, they took us with them to the market to eat. I have no recollection of where that market was and how we ever made it back home, but we did. And we did this for days.

At the end of the compound, there was a high wall as Nassim Hill was several metres higher than our buildings. We would climb the wall to get to Nassim Road. We sometimes turned left to visit the green gardens of mansions of some important people and the guards there chased us away. It was rumoured that the President of Singapore lived there, and that was why we were not allowed to play and roam the gardens. If we turned to the right and walked for some time, we would reach Tanglin Road. At the same location where Tanglin Mall is located today, there was a row of cheap shops where we bought our bottles of Coca-Cola and ice cream. My brother and I could never finish a bottle on our own, so we bought one for the two of us to share. Any way you look at it, each of us got his share of sugar.

During the Jewish holidays, the Israeli community, which in those days must have numbered about a hundred people, gathered at Mrs Moselle Nissim's estate. Mrs Nissim, as we learned to know and call her, was an institution and an anchor for the Jewish and Israeli community in Singapore. I remember her today as a very quiet, smiling elderly woman; there was nothing intimidating about her. We would spend time at the Chesed-El Synagogue, built by her father, but mostly we ran around the huge grassland between the synagogue and her mansion. When we gathered for a holiday dinner on the porch of her home, on arrival, each of us would walk up to Mrs Nissim, who sat on a large armchair in one of her living rooms, shake her hand and greet her. She had a soft and weak handshake; she would smile and nod her head, and seemed pleased to have her estate full of people, especially the loud and noisy children.

For *Pesach*, we received a large shipment of *matzas*. Guests to our house were invited to eat *matza brei* — an omelette with *matza*. My brother would sometimes spend hours in the kitchen preparing *matza brei*. During Europe's winter and early spring, we would receive crates of Jaffa oranges, which were a real feast. These were two of the ways to experience the feeling of home. During the time of the Six Day War in Israel, we only saw movies of the war. We went through the victory albums, but were not there to feel the atmosphere.

After spending three years in Singapore, I moved to Germany for a year before I returned home to Israel. I am pointing this out as living in Frankfurt, Germany, was an entirely different experience from living in Singapore, and I can't today think of a better way to make life in Singapore of the 1960s stand out from a child's experience. In case I failed to make the point, I am reiterating it — Singapore will forever be in my memories synonymous with *freedom*. Exceptional freedom.

Raanan Boral works in a company that organises and manages regional co-operation projects funded by the European Union. He is married with four children and two granddaughters, and lives in a small community in the Judean Hills near Jerusalem, Israel.

Building Venture Capital to Promote Innovation, Economic Growth and Development: Government Efforts in Singapore and Israel

Robyn Klingler-Vidra

Introduction

In newly-established Singapore in 1965, the fledgling army was in desperate need of training. How would they organise their military? Part of the answer — which proved to be a core component of much of the Lion City's modus operandi in the decades that followed — was to learn from others. The Israeli experience was identified by government leaders as a good example: Israel had just established its already well-functioning army following the state's creation in 1948. Being a state of comparable population size and similarly located among neighbours who were less than keen on its existence meant Israel would be a useful teacher. Singaporean politicians knew the problem of the optics of learning from the Jewish state. As Lee Kuan Yew wrote in his 2000 autobiography: "to disguise their presence, we called them 'Mexicans'. They looked swarthy enough." (This was long before the advent of social media, which would have immediately revealed the absurdity of the claim!)

Singaporean venture capital (VC) policy in the early days also drew insights and inspiration from the Israeli model, without much public reference to Israel. Now that has changed, of course, as Israel has come to be known as the Start-up Nation (a name taken from the title of the widely read book by Mr Dan Senor and Mr Saul Singer). From 1992, Vertex, a unit of Temasek, a

Singaporean sovereign wealth fund, was one of the first limited partners in the Israeli chief scientist's VC fund called the Yozma Fund (as will be explained, Singapore came to purposefully adapt Yozma twice). Then in 1997, the two governments launched the Singapore–Israel Industrial R&D Foundation (SIIRD), a bilateral funding initiative between the Singapore Economic Development Board and the Israel Innovation Authority. The Singaporean and Israeli governments now send high-profile delegations to each other's country, and even talk about their long-established military co-operation. On 20 February 2017, Israeli Prime Minister Benjamin Netanyahu made the first-ever official state visit to Singapore, remarking: "Israel and Singapore are innovation nations and, together, we can bring more prosperity for both and a better life for our people and beyond our people, in the neighbourhood for which we live."

There are good reasons for Singaporean policymakers to study Israel's policies to advance venture capital. By 2000, Israel was one of the world's VC powerhouses, both in absolute and per capita terms. In absolute terms, Israel was second only to the United States in its VC market until China's spectacular rise in recent years. According to PwC's 2019 "State of Innovation" report, Israel remains the world's greatest VC cluster on a population basis, with US$674 per capita as of 2018 (compare this with around US$200 in the United States). What's more, 2018 was a record-setting year for the Start-up Nation. Israeli tech companies raised US$6.47 billion in venture capital funding, across 623 deals. More than the eye-popping amount raised, analysts point to the growth in the number of "mega deals" in Israeli VC, with more than 24 deals worth US$50 million or more, according to IVC Research. This helps rebut the longstanding criticism that Israeli tech managers sold too quickly, and that Israeli VCs invested only small sums early on. The Start-up Nation's venture capital market is mature, just as Israeli start-ups have demonstrated their ability to become "unicorns", the term for private companies with valuations in excess of US$1 billion.

Singapore, too, has built a formidable VC market, and is the clear leader in Southeast Asia. It is now home to several unicorns, including Grab, Sea Ltd and Lazada. Its start-ups capture two-thirds of all the venture capital funding going into Southeast Asia, and, similarly, Singapore is the lead domicile for VC funds investing in the region. In 2018, US$3.16 billion of VC money was invested in Southeast Asia, up from US$2.7 billion in 2017. Internationally, Singapore's sovereign wealth funds — GIC and Temasek — are prolific VC investors. According to 2018 PitchBook data, GIC had collectively made 77 VC fund commitments and 433 direct VC investments, while Temasek had 41 VC commitments and 442 direct investments. These activity levels place both GIC and Temasek among the top 10 most active sovereign wealth fund investors in VC.

Snapshot Statistics of Israeli and Singaporean VC Markets

Clearly, both Israel and Singapore are exciting global VC hubs. The prominent role of government policy also makes them fascinating cases to study, as policymakers around the world strive to foster local VC markets that bear some of the traits, and hopefully volumes, of these stars. "Venture capital states" are desired as this high-powered form of early-stage equity finance

	Israel	Singapore
VC deals (US$ in 2018)	US$6.47 billion	US$2.1 billion*
Number of VC managers (As of May 2019 on Crunchbase)	162	195
Notable unicorns	Mobileye, Waze, Houzz, Wix, OrCam, Fiverr	Grab, Lazada, Sea Ltd

*Based on total Southeast Asia VC funding for 2018 at US$3.16 billion (SVCA data, October 2018) and separate data from Vertex and Preqin (October 2018) that Singaporean start-ups received 67 per cent of that money.

is said to help drive innovation advances that bring essential productivity gains and the creation of high-value jobs.[1] Venture capitalists constitute "smart money" as they use their technical expertise and robust professional networks to source potentially high-growth companies, and then use their expertise and networks to help that company grow into a market disruptor; technology companies like Google, Facebook and Amazon all received VC input in their ascent. VC policies are purposeful efforts to promote a local VC market, through the use of enabling regulations, tax treatments (either tax rates or subsidies) and/or funding. More importantly, VC policy does not include the broader swathe of efforts to promote a local entrepreneurial cluster; VC policy is just one part of such efforts. This chapter offers crucial insights into the historic efforts to build VC markets in both Israel and Singapore, including the diffusion of Israel's VC policy to Singapore. The findings are based upon primary interviews with lead VC policymakers in both countries, held between 2011 and 2018, as well as extensive reviews of government reports, policies and communiques.

Israel: VC Policy to Become *the* Start-up Nation

Israel's big push in VC came in the early 1990s, with the famed Yozma Fund (*yozma* means "initiative" in Hebrew). As former Chief Scientist Orna Barry pithily remarked: "Before Elvis there was no rock and roll. Before Yozma, there was no venture capital in Israel." The evolution of government efforts to promote the high-risk asset class is tied up with ambitions of linking Israeli start-ups with American investors and multinationals. This orientation evolved from the late 1960s, when local entrepreneurs and investors had initiated relationships with leaders in the burgeoning VC industry, such as Frederick Adler in New York. These collaborations allowed an Israeli technology firm, Elscient, to list on the Nasdaq Stock Market as early as 1972, less than a year after the Nasdaq was founded. Later, in the early 1980s,

---

[1] Robyn Klingler-Vidra, *The Venture Capital State: The Silicon Valley Model in East Asia* (Ithaca: Cornell University Press, 2018), p. 2.

Yitzchak Yaakov, Israel's chief scientist at the time, created "a specific set of legal entities to use a US tax shelter to channel finance into Israeli ICT firms".[2] This "special ad hoc LP (Limited Partner) program" operated between 1980 and 1986 as a means of channelling US investors to Israeli start-ups.[3] By the 1980s, these strategies had created a small, but thriving information and communications technology (ICT) industry, and one oriented towards international, particularly American, linkages.

Despite this orientation towards international capital and consumer markets, the first concerted effort towards establishing an Israeli VC market had a distinctively domestic tinge. The Inbal Program, launched in 1991 by the Ministry of Finance, was a government insurance scheme that provided a 70 per cent guarantee to four VC funds listed on the Tel Aviv Stock Exchange.[4] The stock exchange lacked sufficient volume — and therefore liquidity — to support exits. Owing to its misfit, when the programme did not produce returns, it was quickly wound down.[5] The next year, the Office of the Chief Scientist's externally focused Yozma Fund went on to catalyse an internationally linked VC market for Israel.

In June 1992, Israel's Office of the Chief Scientist created Yozma Venture Capital Ltd with US$100 million in assets under management. Yozma was led by Mr Yigal Erlich, Israel's chief scientist at that time, with the goal of building an internationally linked, professional venture capital market. Yozma invested via 10 drop-down funds and also made direct investments in start-up companies. The Yozma Fund required the local Israeli VC managers to have foreign partners (e.g., Walden, an American private equity firm and

---

[2]   Dan Breznitz, *Innovation and the State: Political Choices and Strategies for Growth in Israel, Taiwan, and Ireland* (New Haven: Yale University Press, 2007), p. 65.

[3]   Gil Avnimelech, Martin Kenney, and Morris Teubal, "The life cycle model for the creation of national venture capital industries: The US and Israeli experiences", in *Clusters Facing Competition: The Importance of External Linkages*, edited by Elisa Giuliani, Roberta Rabellotti, and Meine Pieter van Dijk (London: Ashgate, 2005), p. 29.

[4]   Gil Avnimelech and Morris Teubal, "Strength of Market Forces and the Successful Emergence of Israel's Venture Capital Industry: Insights from a Policy-led Case of Structural Change", *Revue Economique* 55, no. 6 (2004): 1268.

[5]   Yigal Erlich, interview by author, Tel Aviv, 6 October 2013.

Kyocera in Japan) before they were eligible to receive the money in an effort to bring foreign venture capitalists' investment expertise and network of contacts to Israel.[6] The Yozma Fund was designed to be privatised within five years, so as not to become a subsidy to the VC market. Its participants were given the option to buy out the government investment at cost plus a nominal interest rate and a 5–7 per cent share in the future profits of portfolio company exits. All but one of the funds used that option and bought out the government share.[7]

Through this one-time injection, the Yozma Fund initiated the growth of the Israeli VC market, which became the second biggest VC market in the world on an absolute basis and the world's largest in per capita terms by 2000.

Singapore: Innovating Policy Based upon Learning from Global Leaders

By the mid-1990s, Singaporean policymakers' overall objective was clear: to build a local version of the Silicon Valley innovation clusters. Singapore's then-Deputy Prime Minister Tony Tan set up a ministerial committee to conceive of, and oversee, the Technopreneurship 21 initiative. The committee's explicit aim was precisely "to encourage entrepreneurs to commercialise technology to develop another Silicon Valley or Taiwan".[8] After establishing its goal, members made numerous study trips. According to Mr KC Low, who was the head of funding programmes for the committee, the aim of these trips was to "distil the essence of what the countries have done right, and then adapt it to the Singaporean context". Going well beyond what can be learned in a study trip, Mr Low lived in Silicon Valley in 1996 and 1997

---

[6] Josh Lerner, *Boulevard of Broken Dreams: Why Public Efforts to Boost Entrepreneurship and Venture Capital Have Failed — and What to Do About It* (Princeton: Princeton University Press, 2009), p. 156.

[7] Robyn Klingler-Vidra, Martin Kenney, and Dan Breznitz, "Policies for Financing Entrepreneurship through Venture Capital: Learning from the Successes of Israel and Taiwan", *International Journal of Innovation and Regional Development 7*, no. 3 (2016): 210.

[8] Augustine HH Tan, "*Official Efforts to Attract FDI: Case of Singapore's EDB*", paper presented at the 1999 EWC/KDI Conference on Industrial Globalization in the 21st Century: Impact and Consequences for East Asia and Korea, East West Center, Hawaii, 2–3 August 1999, p. 12.

to ensure he thoroughly understood the model. Upon his return, Mr Low "knew that Singapore had to use different, more specific techniques, to advance its VC market [than the US had]".[9]

This led him and his colleagues to study the Israeli model; he heard that through the provision of direct finance to a cohort of local investors, the Israeli Office of the Chief Scientist had succeeded in catapulting the rise of a thriving local VC market. They had first become aware of the Israeli Yozma initiative because Vertex Venture Holdings, a subsidiary of Temasek, was one of the original LPs to participate in the Yozma Fund. Technopreneurship 21 committee policymakers then conducted study trips to Israel to learn more about Yozma. As a result of these trips, and their subsequent communications with the Israeli Chief Scientist Office, the committee "learned from Israel how to bring the private sector in" so that the fund of VC funds initiative (the TIF) would "not just [be] comprised of government money".[10]

The committee, led by Mr Low for financing initiatives, designed Singapore's fund of VC funds, the TIF, as a purposeful adaptation of the Yozma Fund. The TIF's role was "to develop the VC industry by investing in local and overseas funds, with the intent of accessing deal flows and attracting them and their investee companies to Singapore".[11] The aim of attracting foreign investors to the TIF was to "make strategic investments in leading venture capital firms around the world, to promote the formation of indigenous fund management firms, *encourage foreign venture capital firms to set up operations in Singapore*, and in the process catalyse knowledge transfer and network development through overseas portfolio funds".[12] In this way, "unlike the Israeli Yozma Fund that focused exclusively on supporting domestic VC managers, the larger TIF was designed to attract world class

---

[9] KC Low, interview by author, Singapore, 12 September 2012.

[10] Ibid.

[11] EDB, *Singapore Enterprise Ecosystem: EDB Annual Report 2001–2* (Singapore: EDB, 2002), p. 50.

[12] Winston TH Koh, and Poh Kam Wong, "The Venture Capital Industry in Singapore: A Comparative Study with Taiwan and Israel on the Government's Role", NUS Entrepreneurship Centre Working Papers, WP2005–09 (2005), p. 14. Italics added.

VC managers to Singapore".[13] In that vein, the lion's share (75 per cent) of the TIF's capital went to international VC managers.

As part of the Technopreneurship 21 initiative, policymakers also deployed VC-focused tax credits. In the 1998 budget, the Finance Minister confirmed that tax exemptions for VC funds would be extended on a case-by-case basis for up to five years beyond the maximum of ten years. In addition, Singapore-domiciled VC managers' profits were made eligible for a 10-year tax break (e.g., the tax holiday for pioneer industries) via the Venture Capital Incentive (Section 97) of the Economic Expansion Incentives (Relief from Income Tax) Act.[14] Further tax incentives have been deployed to help reduce VC investors' downside risk. The Standards, Productivity, and Innovation Board offered the Enterprise Investment Incentives Scheme for start-up investors, including VC managers. The scheme allowed venture capitalists to deduct losses incurred against their taxable income. In addition, the Technopreneurship Investment Incentive Scheme offered an allowance for tax deductions (up to 100 per cent of equity invested) on losses from selling qualifying shares or liquidating investments in start-ups.

On the regulatory front, through the 1990s, there was no LP structure available in Singapore. Policymakers felt that they already offered private companies, including VC management firms, an attractive regulatory environment via the private company limited structure (which is notated as Pte Ltd). In the wake of the Dotcom Crash in the early 2000s, they came to a different conclusion about the value of a structure similar in name, not only function, to the United States. In that year, Singapore adopted the LP structure as an effort to be "obviously familiar to international, especially American investors, by having a VC fund structure that is the same in name and in function" as the LP structure popular in Silicon Valley.

Policymakers at Singapore's National Research Foundation (NRF) studied the Israeli fund of VC funds model (Yozma) again when conducting research

---

[13] Low, interview.
[14] Ibid.

on how to address a more specific gap in equity financing. This research was conducted under the umbrella of the National Innovation and Enterprise Framework for the Next Stage of Economic Growth in 2008. NRF Chairman Tony Tan visited Israel with the intention of learning to better formulate Singapore's second fund of VC funds. Dr Tan shared what the delegation had learnt about the Israeli Yozma Fund and its impact:

> *In the early 1990s, the Office of the [Israeli] Chief Scientist also en-*
> *sured that start-up companies have a fair chance of receiving venture*
> *capital funding at its early stage of growth. This was done by creating*
> *a number of early stage venture funds to invest in Israeli start-ups.*
> *In addition to providing this much needed source of funding, this*
> *program ultimately resulted in the development of a healthy venture*
> *capital industry in Israel.[15]*

Following their study of the Israeli model (again), in 2008, NRF launched the Early-Stage Venture Fund (ESVF) to catalyse the set-up of several early-stage VC funds. The ESVF was conceptualised as a new version of an old idea — a new version of the TIF effectively — that is more focused on domestic VC firms. The ESVF was created to address the lack of funding available to Singaporean start-ups at the Series A and B rounds.

Even though it was structured to be more similar to the Yozma model, the ESVF was again deliberately adjusted away from the Israeli model. As mentioned, the Yozma Fund gave its private investors the opportunity to buy out their investment at cost, plus a nominal interest rate and a 7 per cent share in future portfolio company profits. The ESVF, instead, offered a straightforward buyout at 1.25 times the NRF's initial investment. While most of the VCs that participated in the first version of the ESVF — Bioveda

---

[15] National Research Foundations, "Press Release: Singapore to develop a national innovation and enterprise framework for the next stage of economic growth", 10 January 2018, https://www.nrf.gov.sg/docs/default-source/modules/pressrelease/201306251939524540-Israel-trip-press-release-(FINAL).pdf.

Capital, Extream Ventures, New Asia Investments, Raffles Venture Partners — were local, the first batch of VCs also included a blue-chip international VC manager — Walden International. The mostly domestic funds were required to invest in local start-ups.

In September 2013, the ESVF terms were changed to encourage multinational corporations (MNCs) to participate. They changed the requirements to open participation to international VC managers, as this was "a formula that they were more comfortable with".[16] The NRF made the change yet again to attract more investment firms to set up in the country. In line with this aim, the participants in the second ESVF included internationally acclaimed VC managers, including Walden International (the American VC firm that was included in ESVF I) and Tembusu ICT fund (a Japanese VC manager).

Only in September 2015 did the ESVF, in its third instalment, focus on local investors. The ESVF II was announced with S$40 million to link large local enterprises with local start-ups through a corporate VC design. It opened a call for Singaporean firms with corporate venture funds to help grow the local tech ecosystem. The result of the call was the allocation of S$10 million each to the following Singaporean firms' corporate VC arms: CapitaLand Limited, DeClout Limited, Wilmar International Limited, and YCH Group Pte Ltd. This iteration of the ESVF is the first one allocated to Singaporean-headquartered MNCs with the mandate of investing in local start-ups.

In 2017, the government consolidated schemes to support start-ups into a single entity called "Startup SG". While the various programmes, "Talent", "Founder" and "Tech", for instance, focus on finance and other support for start-ups, Startup SG also provides co-investment alongside VC firms based in Singapore, to the tune of a 7:3 ratio for up to S$250,000 investment in a general tech start-up, and S$500,000 for a "deep tech" start-up. The roll-out

---

[16] Low, interview.

of Startup SG is the culmination of disparate efforts to support start-ups and early-stage equity finance that were operating across the government.[17]

Conclusion

Both the Israeli and Singaporean VC markets benefited from purposeful government action. In the Israeli case, the chief scientist's 1992 Yozma Fund created an initial cohort of high-quality VC managers who were linked to international investors. The Yozma Fund built on the already established success of tech start-ups listed on Nasdaq from the 1970s as well as the alignment with American regulations and VC leaders. The Singaporean government initiated VC activities, initially within the Economic Development Board from the early 1990s, and then with contributions from a number of government entities, including the NRF and now Startup SG. In the late 1990s, the government catapulted efforts to develop a domestic VC market, in the shape of the Yozma-inspired S$1 billion Technopreneurship Investment Fund and an onslaught of tax incentives and guarantees; the strategy was distinct from Israel's. For Singaporean policymakers, it was about attracting world-class venture capitalists to the city-state as a means of building up both human and financial capital. Since then, the government has surgically increased and dampened levers for particular segments of VC, through providing more or less generous funding and tax incentives.

Altogether, as in the Silicon Valley case, the Israeli and Singaporean governments have been key protagonists in the ascent of their vibrant VC markets. These "venture capital states" have provided essential funding and enabled regulatory and tax offerings. Crucially, they formulated policies to fit with the "contextual rationality" of their environments, both in terms of the beliefs of their policymakers and in terms of particular gaps and opportunities.[18] Singapore's responsiveness to feedback that they had too

---

[17] For more details on the various Startup SG schemes, see the website of Startup SG, https://www.startupsg.net/programmes/4895/startup-sg-equity.

[18] Klingler-Vidra, *Venture*, pp. 17–20.

much, and too little, funding in the ecosystem has contributed to the policies' effectiveness. The ESVF has been reformulated to specifically address a gap in the early-stage "A Round" and then to entice large Singaporean companies to invest in VC. Startup SG was created to streamline government efforts to support its growing tech start-up ecosystem. The thoughtfulness and responsiveness of government efforts have paid off. These local VC pools, in turn, provide "smart money" to start-ups such as the growing number of unicorns in both Israel and Singapore.

Bibliography

Avnimelech, Gil, Martin Kenney, and Morris Teubal. "The life cycle model for the creation of national venture capital industries: the US and Israeli experiences". In *Clusters Facing Competition: The Importance of External Linkages,* edited by Elisa Giuliani, Roberta Rabellotti, and Meine Pieter van Dijk, pp. 195–214. London: Ashgate, 2005.

Avnimelech, Gil, and Morris Teubal. "Strength of Market Forces and the Successful Emergence of Israel's Venture Capital Industry: Insights from a Policy-led Case of Structural Change". *Revue Economique* 55, no. 6 (2004): 1265–1300.

Breznitz, Dan. *Innovation and the State: Political Choices and Strategies for Growth in Israel, Taiwan, and Ireland.* New Haven: Yale University Press, 2007.

EDB. *Singapore's Enterprise Ecosystem: EDB Annual Report 2001–2.* Singapore: EDB, 2002.

Erlich, Yigal. "The Yozma Program — Success Factors and Policy." Presentation, Yozma Group, Tel Aviv, Israel, 2 January 2013.

Klingler-Vidra, Robyn, Martin Kenney, and Dan Breznitz. "Policies for Financing Entrepreneurship through Venture Capital: Learning from the Successes of Israel and Taiwan". *International Journal of Innovation and Regional Development* 7, no. 3 (2016): 203–21.

Klingler-Vidra, Robyn. *The Venture Capital State:Tthe Silicon Valley Model in East Asia.* Ithaca: Cornell University Press, 2018.

Koh, Winston T.H., and Poh Kam Wong. "The Venture Capital Industry in Singapore: A Comparative Study with Taiwan and Israel on the Government's Role". NUS Entrepreneurship Centre Working Papers, WP2005–09, (2005).

Lee, Kuan Yew. *From Third World to First: Singapore and the Asian Economic Boom.* New York: HarperCollins, 2000.

Lerner, Josh. *Boulevard of Broken Dreams: Why Public Efforts to Boost Entrepreneurship and Venture Capital Have Failed — and What to Do About It.* Princeton: Princeton University Press, 2009.

National Research Foundation, "Press Release: Singapore to develop a national innovation and enterprise framework for the next stage of economic growth", 10 January 2018, https://www.nrf.gov.sg/docs/default-source/modules/pressrelease/201306251939524540-Israel-trip-press-release-(FINAL).pdf.

Senor, Dan, and Saul Singer. *Start-up Nation: The Story of Israel's Economic Miracle.* New York: Hachette, 2009.

Tan, Augustine HH. "Official Efforts to Attract FDI: Case of Singapore's EDB". Paper presented at the 1999 EWC/KDI Conference on Industrial Globalization in the 21st Century: Impact and Consequences for East Asia and Korea. East West Center, Hawaii, 2–3 August 1999.

Robyn Klingler-Vidra is a senior lecturer in political economy at King's College London.

Translating Research into Real-World Innovation: Experiences of Israel and Singapore

Mark Shmulevich

Ask anyone about Israel today and "innovation" would be cited by many people as one of the first things that come to mind. This tiny country has managed to produce numerous innovative products, from cherry tomatoes to flash drives, instant messaging software ICQ and GPS navigation software Waze to internet firewalls. These inventions were non-conventional and, over a short period of time, they have proven to be globally competitive and commercially successful.

What is less known is that many Israeli inventions are often the result of academic research, and that there are mechanisms in the country that support moving research findings to the marketplace for financial return and global impact. These systems work well and bring results.

Everywhere in the world, there is a cultural gap between industry and academia. Israel and Singapore are no exceptions. These two areas of human activity are so different that they sometimes seem impossible to bridge. In the classical academic tradition, the goal of research is creating knowledge. Researchers have practical goals, both in their projects and their career in general; however, these goals fall mostly within the academic domain. Open research and, to some extent, freedom of choosing what to do are essential in the academic world. In contrast, industry targets are usually practical and applied. The ultimate goal is creating wealth, growing shareholder value more than social value. New products on top of new knowledge are essential to achieve that. Hence, industry and academia have long been treated as two different worlds, and fostering the translation of academic research into real-world technologies has not been seen as an essential goal.

In 1925, the first technology transfer office (TTO) appeared in the United States. A group of nine alumni of the University of Wisconsin-Madison set up the Wisconsin Alumni Research Foundation (WARF) with an initial operating budget of US$900, one hundred dollars from each of them. In its initial years, it was largely focused on commercialising a single research project, using vitamin D to cure rickets. However, the concept of a full-scale university TTO was born soon after.

Technology Transfer in the Start-up Nation

Twenty-five years later, this concept of technology transfer was tested and refined in Israel, when the Weizmann Institute of Science and the Hebrew University of Jerusalem created their TTOs. Today, these organisations alone account for dozens of thousands of patents and hundreds of spin-off companies, including Mobileye (an early pioneer of vision systems that allow vehicles to recognise hazards, acquired by Intel for US$15.7 billion), RSA (one of the first public-key cryptosystems, acquired by EMC for US$2.1 billion) and Mazor (a medical device company and manufacturer of robotic guidance systems for spinal surgery, acquired by Medtronic for US$1.64 billion).

The Israeli technology transfer network consists of fifteen main nodes, nine of which are linked to universities and research centres, while the remaining six are at hospitals or health maintenance organisations. Several of them have generated cumulatively over US$10 billion in sales each. Every year, about 150 new technologies are licensed from Israeli universities and research institutions, while dozens of new companies are spun off from academic research.

What were the main rules that determined the efficiency of TTOs in Israel? And how to explain that, while the research budget of the Israel

Institute of Technology (Technion) is less than 10 per cent of that of the TTO at Massachusetts Institute of Technology (MIT), their incomes from their commercialisation of research do not differ significantly?

The commercialisation policy in Israel is generally the same across most of the academic institutes in the country. Unless the invention is done by undergraduate students, the institution owns the intellectual property rights. The inventor, co-inventors and students receive around 50 per cent of the commercialisation benefits. There are two channels of commercialisation: licensing of the intellectual property or founding a new company based on the technology in question, with or without the inventors in the executive team.

Start-ups are well accepted in Israel and there is a positive culture towards them. Start-ups serve as a bridge between research and corporations, and de-risk technologies. Other features of Israeli society which make the adoption of start-up culture in the research environment an easier task include a common intention to work fast to see the practical results of what one does. In Israeli academia, the share of researchers who want to create working technology and a successful business out of their research is seemingly more than anywhere else in the world. Many of them dream not of building a successful business, but of becoming a serial entrepreneur. One regularly meets such researchers inside the Israeli academic circles. Successful exits of start-ups from academia serve as positive reinforcement of the whole process. Besides academia, another source of innovation is the Israeli military; people serving in its technology units establish companies in cybersecurity, engineering and many other areas. Founders of such companies are usually result-oriented, knowledgeable and efficient.

In Israel, technology transfer companies have a strong business focus and are run separately, with business people on their boards, as opposed to being university departments. They have a business mentality and serve as a one-stop shop for start-ups, consulting them and bringing the mature industry and investor connections to the young companies.

Let's look at a few examples of already commercialised research projects as well as those with a strong technology innovation potential.

Mobileye Vision Technologies provides warnings to drivers to prevent collisions on the road. The company was founded in 1999 on technology developed by Professor Amnon Shashua of the Hebrew University and was commercialised by Yissum, the university's TTO. Mobileye, which has existed as a subsidiary of the Hebrew University since its founding, later developed a number of proprietary algorithms on which the company's driver assistant technology is now based. In July 2013, Mobileye raised US$400 million in a deal that valued the company at US$1.5 billion and attracted some large US investors. It was then acquired by Intel.

At Tel Aviv University, researchers have created the world's first 3D-printed heart, made using cells and biological material from a human patient. The project is a significant step forward for the field of regenerative medicine; it is the first time that anyone, anywhere has successfully engineered and printed an entire heart replete with cells, blood vessels, ventricles and chambers. Patented biomaterials serve as the bio-inks, substances made of sugars and proteins that can be used for 3D-printing of complex tissue models. Despite this potential, the 3D-printed heart is still far from being ready for transplantation into humans because, at this stage, the 3D-printed heart is smaller than required for human transplant. But the next phase of research and engineering is expected to close this gap.

The uniqueness of Israel's history and the concentration of high-tech and entrepreneurial talent have led to the country being an example of an open innovation boot camp. The proximity of innovative institutions in Israel creates a certain buzz. People from different fields work together with one another. Many of them move between academia, military, research and development (R&D), venture capital and even policymaking. At some points, they may even wear several hats at once.

The venture capital industry in Israel received a strong boost in the 1990s when a key government programme, Yozma (which means "initiative" in Hebrew), was launched. In its 2010 report, the Organisation for Economic

Cooperation and Development (OECD) described Yozma as "the most successful and original programme in Israel's relatively long history of innovation policy". The programme invested around US$80 million for stakes in ten new venture capital funds and set up its own fund to invest directly in start-ups. Nine of its fifteen portfolio companies went public or were acquired. Over the 1990s, the total venture capital investment in Israel grew almost 60 times to over US$3 billion.

The Technological Incubators Program by the Israel Innovation Authority was the other government-led effort that helped the start-up ecosystem further develop. It started in 1991, partly designed to provide new immigrants from the former Soviet Union, one-third of whom were skilled engineers and scientists, with the capital and resources to become successful entrepreneurs in Israel. It has since expanded into 24 incubators. The start-ups under the Technological Incubators Program receive both funding and mentorship. Most of the funding may come in the form of a grant.

The Lion City's Experience

In Singapore, research commercialisation as a topic of significant attention developed later than in Israel. The Republic started investing significant funds in research in the 1980s. Multinational technology companies at the same time successfully tested the technical capabilities of Singapore and started to establish worldwide product charters in the country in the 1990s. For example, HP Singapore designed and developed the Jornada pocket personal computers and launched R&D in the areas of inkjet printing technologies in the city-state. Seagate researched and then designed its U series disk drive in the Singapore Science Park, achieving a density of over 32Gb per square inch, a record at that time.

Today, Singapore is a favoured location for multinational companies. More than 7,000 companies have some form of headquarters (HQs) in the city-state, and many of these businesses run R&D in Singapore. The number of Singapore-headquartered businesses is considerably more than those in Hong Kong, Sydney, Shanghai or Tokyo, most of which host fewer than 1,000 HQs, with the exception of Hong Kong (over 1,300 as of 2017).

In the 1980s, research was mainly conducted at the universities in Singapore. It was only in the late 1980s that A*Star, the Agency for Science, Technology and Research (formerly known as the National Science and Technology Board), established its first mission-oriented research institutes. It made important contributions in developing much-needed human capital and core capabilities in multidisciplinary research areas, many of which had strong commercialisation potential. Intellectual property licensing became a primary model of commercialisation of research at the universities and institutes. Experience in working with industry on commercial projects received during the 1990s and later through contract R&D projects was of great use in that process.

An example of early collaborations was the joint work between A*Star-funded Gintic Institute of Manufacturing Technology and MMI Holdings Ltd, a local company supporting multinational corporation (MNC) manufacturers in Singapore that started in 1998. It resulted in the establishment of the first magnesium die-casting plant in Southeast Asia in 1999.

Over the next decade, the research that was conducted at Singapore's institutes of higher learning, as well as institutes of A*Star, led to a growing stack of intellectual property and scientific findings. Coupled with the excellent quality of education in Singapore and the growing availability of investments in the country that may go to the research-based start-ups, these became the foundation for the future growth of a number of successful research commercialisation cases.

Let's look at quantum technologies, one of the areas in which translation of research into business spin-offs is happening now across the world. The first applications in areas such as secure communication have already become commercial projects. The other application areas, such as quantum computing, are quickly advancing; quantum systems that have been constructed in recent years are already large and stable enough for researchers to observe their behaviour and work with them in the real world.

In Singapore, the Centre for Quantum Technologies was established in 2007 as one of the few national Research Centres of Excellence, aimed at bringing together physicists, computer scientists, and engineers to do basic research on quantum physics and to build devices based on quantum phenomena. The Centre has demonstrated strong research results. In recent years, commercialisation has started too. Several quantum spin-offs from the Centre received investments. Among them are Atomionics, a start-up that builds atom interferometry-based sensing systems for navigation and exploration that will work reliably and accurately everywhere — including underwater, underground and other GPS-denied areas — and Horizon Quantum Computing, a start-up working on a new generation of software development tools for the quantum era.

Quantum technology commercialisation is getting additional support these days in Israel as well. A new nation-wide Quantum Initiative is launching soon. It is expected to last for six years. Among the new programme goals will be the support of novel application development in areas such as quantum sensing, communication, materials, computing, and simulation.

The technology commercialisation scene in Singapore has developed significantly since 2000. It now includes players such as SGInnovate, a government agency that, among other things, works with entrepreneurial scientists to build deep tech start-ups and also nurtures the communities that bring researchers, investors and entrepreneurs together.

Several universities in Singapore have TTOs too. NTUitive is the TTO at Nanyang Technological University (NTU). The TTO at the National

University of Singapore is NUS Industry Liaison Office (ILO), which is part of NUS Enterprise. Both universities were ranked best in Asia and joint 11th globally in the 2020 QS World University Rankings.[1]

NUS Enterprise's history goes back to 1988, when the NUS Entrepreneurship Centre was established as a university-level centre called the Centre for Management of Innovation and Technopreneurship. In 2001, it was renamed NUS Entrepreneurship Centre (NEC). It was established as part of NUS Enterprise to nurture entrepreneurial learning and venture creation among the NUS community. NUS ILO manages the university's technology transfer and promotes research collaborations with industry and partners. ILO manages NUS's intellectual property, commercialises its intellectual assets and facilitates the spinning-off of technologies into start-up companies. In 2018, NUS ILO launched the new Graduate Research Innovation Program (Grip) that is aimed at enabling PhD students and researchers at NUS to develop and create start-ups while continuing to work with NUS in academia.

NTUitive, a part of the young and research-intensive NTU ranked first among the world's best young universities in the 2020 QS Top 50 Under 50 World Rankings, was established much later than NUS Enterprise, in 2014.[2] NTUitive is responsible for managing the intellectual property assets of the university and to help take technology from the lab to the marketplace. In addition, NTUitive focuses on developing the innovation ecosystem. At the same time, it supports the university's mission to make innovation and entrepreneurship a defining feature of the university's brand of education. Some of the areas in which NTUitive has worked in recent years include 3D-printing, energy and batteries, and medicine.

---

[1] For more information on the QS World University Rankings, visit: https://www.topuniversities.com/university-rankings/world-university-rankings/2020.

[2] For more information on the QS Top 50 Under 50 World Rankings, visit: https://www.topuniversities.com/university-rankings-articles/top-50-under-50-next-50-under-50/qs-top-50-under-50-2020.

In 2007, the Singapore-MIT Alliance for Research and Technology (SMART) was established as a joint enterprise between MIT and Singapore's National Research Foundation (NRF). The SMART Innovation Centre operates under SMART and is funded by the NRF. Similar to the highly successful Deshpande Center for Technological Innovation at MIT, the SMART Centre aims to bring the market definition closer to technology development by having each selected project worked on by a team that, in addition to the researchers, includes either an entrepreneur or a venture capitalist right from the start.

The funding part of the innovation ecosystem in Singapore has also grown substantially over the last five to seven years. The Singapore government has provided much assistance to boost this part of the ecosystem. Various venture funds, some of which are supported by government co-investment schemes, operate in the country. Availability of capital ready to go into early-stage technology in Singapore is no longer a limiting factor for technology entrepreneurs, including the researchers who are considering spinning-off start-ups.

New organisations working on applied technologies continue to regularly launch in Singapore. Satellite Technology and Research Centre (STAR), jointly launched by NUS Engineering and the DSO National Laboratories in 2018, is an example. The Centre develops distributed satellite systems, with a focus on flying multiple small satellites in formation or a constellation. Such centres might work as bridges between the research and commercial application in the respective areas in Singapore. In this case, STAR aims to become a hub for research, education and commercialisation of expertise and technologies relating to the space industry in the country.

Another example is a new pilot plant to treat industrial wastewater that was launched in 2019. It may help to potentially reduce the amount of liquid waste by over 90 per cent and also recover precious metals from the treated water which can then be sold and reused. The plant is being built jointly by the Separation Technologies Applied Research and Translation (START) Centre, a national-level facility to develop and commercialise innovative separation and filtration technologies, and Memsift Innovations Pte Ltd, a local water technology firm specialising in zero-liquid discharge water treatment systems. The START Centre is supported by Singapore's Economic Development Board (EDB) and NTU, being a part of NTUitive.

In 2015, LUX Photonics Consortium was established in Singapore as an initiative by NTU and NUS, supported by the NRF. Its vision is to serve as a catalyst and a networking platform to translate cutting-edge research in photonics into diverse applications underpinned by the value chain created. As in other examples, the mission of this centre includes leveraging research and resources in the institutes of higher learning for the industry. After three years of operations, the results of LUX consortium's work include supporting various industrial projects, from start-ups, such as Nanoveu, which specialises in nanotechnology applications, including high-tech screen protectors allowing long-sighted people to see clear images on digital devices without glasses, to others such as Palomar, a US-headquartered assembly machine manufacturer, which launched an R&D centre in Singapore in 2018 with the consortium's help.

The government plays a key role in the technology ecosystem development in Singapore. Agencies such as NRF, EDB, Infocomm and Media Development Authority, and SGInnovate are among the government actors in this field. The commercial players in Singapore have not been as strongly involved in the commercialisation ecosystem. But it is changing now, with a large number of new venture capital funds working in the country and more and more MNCs looking at the start-ups and university partnerships.

Thinking about the Future

What should we focus on to help more research projects turn into technologies and businesses? Below are a few ideas.

How universities treat the translation of academic research into industry plays a paramount role in the success of technology commercialisation. The best universities are reinventing themselves, becoming local environments for innovation, entrepreneurship and industrial leadership. Increasingly, a university that has serious academic achievements but cannot demonstrate its impact on the marketplace is seen as potentially becoming less relevant in the future.

Both in Singapore and Israel, this risk is well understood. Two universities from each of these countries have made it to the list of global top-100 universities that were granted the most US utility patents in 2018. Singapore's NTU occupied the highest place — 49th — out of the four universities, which are NTU, NUS, Tel Aviv University and Technion. In the overall patenting activity, Israel was ranked 10th and Singapore 12th out of 140 countries reviewed in the 2018 World Economic Forum Global Competitiveness Report.

Top research universities are adopting some of the best management practices from the corporate world. Partial introduction of business management know-how to the university space helps make technology commercialisation even more efficient.

Israel's approach to the development of TTOs at universities was bottom-up first, and top-down in the later stages. The first TTOs shaped themselves in the best way largely by trial and error. Then the government helped scale the successful TTO models, launching them at other institutions in the country, not only at research universities. This dual-stage approach has turned out to be effective and is considered by many among the most unique features of the long history of the technology commercialisation process in the country.

The spirit of entrepreneurship and the wish to see the practical applications of research are critical for the success of the endeavour to commercialise research. Examples of people who have tried the technology commercialisation journey and achieved great results will motivate many others to try. These examples exist and should be promoted even more.

Entrepreneurs, researchers, businessmen and investors should work closely together to become a single ecosystem in which no technology news will remain unnoticed. The consortia needed for start-up development can be created more easily within than outside of this ecosystem.

Similarly important are the incentives that researchers have for commercialising their technologies. While basic research may be done for the sake of research findings, the government funding of later-stage applied projects may require a commercialisation roadmap as a necessary application package. It will incentivise researchers to plan their work in a way that will make future commercialisation a more probable outcome.

In addition to having university-linked commercialisation companies in place, bringing more business-oriented entities closer to researchers is important since more often than not successful spin-offs are run not (or not only) by researchers, but by business-oriented people. This way, principal investigators remain involved in the business in one of the technology or R&D roles (up to chief technology officer) and as shareholders. However, business management is driven by people with more commercial experience. Researchers will keep doing what they do best (research), while the business of taking the technologies to the next level, which includes business development, fundraising, and many other business-related activities, will be taken care of by another group of people. This is especially important in the generally risk-averse research environment. Hence, fostering the relationship between the business community and the research community could potentially lead to an improved commercialisation scene. Bringing more entrepreneurial people with experience in the tech business to work in Singapore is also important.

Finally, it would be beneficial to have even more vehicles that include good financing engines suitable for early-stage technologies (including sophisticated deep-tech investors) as well as high-level mentoring. There should be a variety of vehicles suitable for different project types. For example, in the pharmaceutical industry, the development cycles are long and a shorter-term funding mechanism will not work.

The approaches of Israel and Singapore to technology commercialisation are both unique. In both countries, the collaboration between the state and civil technology is gaining traction. Being open to best practices and experience exchange, and providing mutual access to the relevant financial vehicles and to international markets, research co-operation and mentoring should remain among the priorities of this growing collaboration. It will support the technology commercialisation ecosystems in both countries and foster more business spin-offs from research, positively benefiting the economies in both countries and our lives.

Mark Shmulevich is chief operating officer at Taiger, an artificial intelligence software company headquartered in Singapore offering pioneering solutions that increase efficiency of information processing at large organisations. Dr Shmulevich also sits on several boards, including SGTech, the technology industry association in Singapore, where he is vice-chairman of the digital transformation chapter, and Zimin Institute for Engineering Solutions Advancing Better Lives at Tel Aviv University, Israel.

Trax: The First Israel–Singapore Unicorn

Joel Bar-El and Dror Feldheim

Mikanna

It all began, like many other beginnings in life, by pure coincidence. It was September 2010. Mika Bar-El and Anna Feldheim, both two years old, started their first day of kindergarten in Singapore. Since both Mika and Anna are Israeli, their parents sent them to Sir Manasseh Meyer International School, where they hoped the girls could learn a bit of Hebrew.

On the first day, Anna's mum, Dalia, took her to school, where she met Mika's mum, Neta, who welcomed her with her huge kind smile and invited the family over for dinner. And from there, it all began.

Mika's parents, Neta and Joel, had relocated to Singapore in 1998 when Joel was 26, following his job opportunity with SunGard Data Systems. Neta, a social worker by profession and 25 years old, followed Joel to the unknown land in the East. They arrived in Singapore as a young newly-wed couple.

When he was in Singapore, Joel was promoted to head of Asia Pacific at SunGard, and after four years, he relocated to New York City to become SunGard's head of North America. After two years in the Big Apple, he left SunGard to open his first start-up, Tersus, a software company, in Israel. Three years later, they relocated back to Singapore to join a new company called SentryI, a wealth management platform which was successfully sold two years later. During those years, the family expanded: Juval was born in 2001 in Singapore, Jonathan in 2004 in Israel, and Mika in 2008 back in Singapore.

Across the globe, Anna's parents, Dalia and Dror Feldheim, also started their ascent up their career ladders in the same year as Joel. In 1998, Dalia, a psychology and business major, received an offer to move to Geneva with Procter and Gamble (P&G). At the same time, Dror graduated with a degree in business and started work as a brand and retail manager in a private equity fund called Expand. The couple had two young children while in Geneva: Mia (2002) and Liam (2003). Then in 2004, Dror had a new boss who was eager to move Dror to Russia, and worked hard to persuade the young couple. A week later, the adventurous duo moved to Moscow with Mia and Liam. After three cold but exciting years, where Dror excelled in retail and Dalia in marketing, they were both promoted and moved back to Geneva where Anna was born (2008). The next opportunity presented itself when Dalia was offered a marketing director role in Singapore and the couple, who were passionate about Asia, decided to move East. In 2010, they arrived in the Land of the Merlion.

So it was in 2010 that the two families, finding each other in Singapore, began to spend more and more time together after that first encounter on Mika and Anna's first day at school. The girls spent so much time together that they got the nickname Mikanna.

Synagogue Inspiration

One night in September, the two couples met for dinner at the Bar-Els', where Joel was testing new dough recipes for the pizza parlour that he and Neta had decided to open. That night, the pizza wasn't too good, but the conversation was, and a friendship between the families was established.

A month later, it was Jewish New Year, and the families decided to meet up at the local synagogue. Built by the Jewish community dating back some 150 years, the synagogue is a great place to mingle with new and local families. Both families are not religious, but they wanted to give their children a taste of their homeland's traditions. But like most non-religious Jews, after praying for a bit, the men went outside and found themselves engaging in deep conversation about business opportunities. There, on the steps of the synagogue, the meeting of two creative minds as well as "divine inspiration" led to the birth of a new company.

Dror shared his retail experience and frustrations with the wastage involved in properly tracking stock, shelf management and promotions. Joel shared that he was consulting a young company, Cam-Trax, on creating image recognition technology for the gaming industry.

Dror thought it would be a huge business opportunity to solve the existing retail execution gaps, and Joel thought he had a technological solution which could solve them — and an idea was born! In one day, Trax — the name and logo — was created. Their idea was to build a company based on computer vision as the core technology which can help businesses fulfil their needs to better track retail shelves to drive turnover and reduce wastage.

We Love Singapore

Why Singapore? If Trax received a 25-cent investment for every time this question was asked, it would have been a unicorn long ago. It seems to be the most commonly asked question by investors, customers and industry partners alike.

There are many answers to this question, but it is safe to say that without being in Singapore, it would have been nearly impossible for Trax to establish itself as a world leader, with A-class investors, global operations, and unicorn status.

We would start with the obvious and most critical element in every successful enterprise: the family. In Trax's case: a wife and three children × 2. Singapore provides a safe haven for families — a common language (English), personal safety, and a world-class education system. This garden city also has lavish condominiums with all sorts of facilities available and lots of family-friendly activities. Singapore is also spouse-friendly and provides easy access to work permits for the "better half".

During her years in Singapore, Neta completed her master's degree, started her doctorate, continued practising as a group facilitator, became a relocation expert and blogger, and managed her own business while also focused on raising and nurturing the family.

Dalia continued her executive career with large enterprises and became a business coach and yoga instructor, travelling extensively around the region and globally. She is now completing her masters at INSEAD.

As the saying goes: "happy wife, happy life". When the basics are well taken care of, the entrepreneur can focus on establishing his company.

Trax was established on 11 November 2010. After spending just a few hours online, the company was formed. Opening a bank account merely took a breezy 30 minutes, most of which was spent waiting in line. While Joel and Dror thought Trax was a unique name, they found out there were more than 50 companies with the word Trax included in their names in Singapore alone.

Singapore has no work visa quotas or barriers for hiring foreign talent in the deep technology sector, apart from educational and salary thresholds, which are logical. Hence, hiring Trax's first employees was easy. And there is plenty of talent in Singapore and Southeast Asia in general to choose from.

Managing the company's finances was also relatively easy. Investors felt comfortable with Singapore's monetary governance and strict laws, and the Singapore dollar is an ultra-stable currency. Its economy is also stable, which is why numerous investors, family offices, venture capital and private equity funds decided to call the city-state home.

Singapore also extends substantial benefits and grants to newly formed start-ups, providing financial aid in the early (and so fragile) years of any new venture.

Furthermore, Singapore enjoys world-class infrastructure, stable high-speed internet and high-end communication systems. Strategically located, Singapore is a mere few hours flight from all major countries in Asia, and about 10–12 hours flight from any major city in Europe.

And last but not least, Singapore has one of the best on-shore tax regimes. There is no capital gains tax (so the founders and investors can realise the full value of their investment tax-free) and it has one of the lowest corporate tax rates globally. As such, Singapore was a great base for Trax to be born, grow and mature.

Beginners' Luck

Besides Joel and Dror, the first employee, Shavit Clein, was hired in April 2011 to lead market development. Trax's first office was a shared office in Suntec City in Singapore. One room, about three by three metres in size. The trio were there for one year before it became too small and they had to move on.

Trax's first external investor was Tamara Minick-Scokalo, Dalia's ex-boss from P&G many years before. Given her proven managerial skills and consumer packaged goods knowledge, Tamara became Trax's first chief executive officer (CEO). Tamara also invested US$350,000 at a price per share of US$0.52 (representing valuation of US$1.5 million).

In December 2010, Joel and Dror learnt that the global innovation head of P&G was visiting Singapore. That was an opportunity not to be missed, and a meeting was arranged. Since the meeting was organised at such short notice, Trax's first business cards were printed about 45 minutes before the meeting began. Unfortunately, the vice-president (VP) was late and his deputy insisted that they start without him. But Dror and Joel applied Israeli *chutzpa* (Yiddish word for audacity) and insisted that they wait. When the VP finally joined the meeting, he was initially angry at the delay. However, as Dror and Joel presented their new vision, the VP's approach slowly changed and later turned to pure delight as their solution (as a vision) was exactly what he was looking for.

The meeting ended well, and it is hard to contemplate where Trax would have been today if it had not. That meeting led eventually to the first pilot with P&G, the largest fast-moving consumer goods company in the world, with all the learning and reputation that came with it.

With a great vision and a first client, it was then time to focus on the computer vision product. The obvious choice was to start in Israel. Besides the fact that both founders are Israeli, Israel is considered a global superpower in computer vision and machine learning at large. The number of Israeli start-ups in this area is by far the largest in the world (per capita) and probably among the top three on an absolute basis. Israel is also ranked first in the world in terms of its investment in research and innovation as a percentage of its gross domestic product (and hence became known as the "Start-up Nation" for that reason).

Trax's first research and development (R&D) centre was thus established in Tel Aviv, physically located in the living room of the first Israeli employee, Paulina Fogel. The team was tasked with creating the first working prototype for a pilot in Venezuela in one month! Using Tersus' unique development language, the team managed to create the infrastructure and the pilot led to 15 per cent sales growth, the first of many such successful pilots in other markets for P&G and later for Coca Cola and other giant consumer packaged goods companies.

In 2012, two years after its establishment, the company had 30 employees and was valued at US$15 million. That year, Dror and Joel were invited to give their first major presentation at a large regional marketing conference with leading industry veterans. When they arrived in Panama after a 32-hour flight, they found out that their presentation on the next day was not at a small booth as was previously agreed. Instead, they had to present in front of a large audience of 1,000 retailers and top executives, and there was a request for a live demo to boot.

Immediately, Joel tried out the demo; all was working well and they went to bed. The next morning, Joel woke up early due to jet lag and decided to try out the demo again. This time, it wasn't working! Pictures uploaded seemed to disappear into cyberspace. It was 5am in Panama. He called up the team in Israel who were still awake and got them working to resolve it, but without success. It was now 6.30am, and the presentation was scheduled for

8am. At 7am, they finally managed to get hold of their coding expert in San Francisco. At 7.30am, he called back. Apparently, there was a coding error on the new website that was designed in honour of the event. Although it was fixed, as the fix needed to be propagated to all the name-server routers of the global internet, it could take anything from minutes up to 24 hours for all systems to be back online. As it was the World Wide Web, its behaviour could not be predicted. The two young men realised then that it was time to pray.

Joel went on stage at 8am to begin his presentation as scheduled. But he tried to stall the demo portion for as long as possible. At 8.25am, they needed to start the demo. Dror was so anxious that he could not watch; instead, he had his eyes shut. Joel, on the other hand, was in a mental bubble of high concentration. He pressed the button, Dror held his breath … and to their surprise and relief, the demo worked flawlessly! That event was a major success.

Dror and Joel arrived back in Singapore on the evening of *Shavuot*, the Jewish name for the Feast of Weeks, and went with their families to the *sukka* (or temporary hut) to celebrate. The rabbi heard about the remarkable events in Panama and invited them for an *aliya* (reading of Torah) on the next day to say *birkat hagomel*, a prayer said when a major disaster is avoided. Divine intervention was at play again.

In late 2012, Joel and Dror met Richard Gati, a Singapore-based angel investor. Trax was looking for another round of financing (US$1 million) and Richard, along with fellow angel investors, invested (at valuation of US$4 million). As it was with the meeting with P&G's global innovation head, it is hard to fathom where Trax would have ended up without this investment. As it turned out, in the next five years, Trax managed to raise an additional US$80 million from this circle of high net worth individuals and family offices, allowing it to skip the need to deal with venture capital firms altogether.

When concluding his first investment in Trax, Richard asked Joel and Dror a direct and surprising question (the same question that would return many times in future rounds): "If someone were to give you 10 million dollars, right here, right now, would you sell the company to him?" Joel and Dror showed good survival instincts by answering simultaneously and convincingly: "No way! We are here to build a billion-dollar company."

After the meeting ended and they were alone, they both confessed that if a real million-dollar cheque was presented before them, they probably would be asking "Where do I sign?". But their resilience and belief in themselves did not let them down. Coincidentally, 18 months later, Trax received its first buy-out offer for US$30 million in cash. The offer was unanimously rejected.

In 2012, Tamara decided to take on another role, while remaining a member of the board. Thus, Joel was appointed officially as Trax's CEO.

From Fair Winds into a Rough Sea

In 2013, Trax signed its first recurring revenue contract. The client was Coca Cola Amatil in Australia. Besides the new relationship with Coca Cola, Trax started to sign contracts with more and more companies globally and with that came an increase in revenue. In 2013, Trax's revenue was US$370,000; in 2014, the company registered revenue of around US$1.5 million, followed by US$5 million in 2015. The company raised additional funding and price per share rose from 52 cents in 2011 to US$7.31 in 2014 with a valuation of US$60 million.

Then, Trax opened its first global subsidiaries. In Tel Aviv, Trax moved out of Paulina's living room into proper offices; in Singapore, Trax rented a shophouse in Chinatown; and in London, a new office was established. Dror and Joel remained a tight-knit duo, and, despite having bigger office space, they insisted on continuing to share a room, which later became a tradition and a symbol of the collaboration and partnership shaping the culture of Trax.

At the end of 2016, the company had 140 employees and about US$11 million in revenue. The company also received its second buy-out proposal, this time for US$180 million, which was also unanimously rejected.

Despite the good momentum, there were also challenges during those years.

Singapore and Israel have very different cultures, especially when it comes to openness to conflict versus the Asian "saving face" mentality. At one meeting, the Israelis were passionately putting forward an argument while the Singaporeans were quietly taking it all in, until Trax's Israeli chief technology officer turned to the Singaporeans and said: "Stop being so polite; in Israel, it's considered rude." That incident was the springboard for a company-wide initiative to bring together the best of both cultures: the openness to talk and raise conflicts, and a home-grown communication methodology to encourage everyone in the discussion to speak their minds openly and respectfully, while living up to the company's values. Its ability to mature as an organisation and to weld together a team across multiple countries, time zones and cultures was how Trax managed to cross the chasm into further growth.

The toll of managing an increasingly larger organisation, with more subsidiaries and employees in all corners of the globe, proved higher than expected. Investors were pushing for ever increasing growth trajectories, and clients became more demanding, expecting customisation and scale, coupled with lower costs.

By 2016, the company had grown to 50 clients in 20 markets. While it continued to grow, it could not meet the ever-increasing demands. After missing revenue projections for a few quarters, there were even questions raised on whether the company had outgrown its founders. A close board vote of 3:2 gave the duo-founders another chance at improving the expected performance.

Despite the rough sea, this little ship sailed on.

A Unicorn in the Making

In 2017, the desired turnaround was achieved. Revenue surged to US$31 million, and private equity firms started to eye the technology company from

Singapore that was fast becoming a global name. Subsidiaries were opened in Brazil, United States and China, and, for the first time, Trax started to invest in its North American expansion, which resulted in a substantial revenue hike. Dror and Joel started "living" on board Singapore Airlines planes, arriving home only on weekends and travelling the rest of the time.

Warburg Pincus invested in Trax in June 2017, and brought a whole new direction to the company's mindset and operations. Jeff Perlman, who represented Warburg on Trax's board of directors, gave Joel a very simple-to-understand direction: US$3 billion valuation in three years. Jeff also pushed the company to start acquiring other companies, which could supplement Trax's offering in new markets and with new products.

By the end of 2017, the company had made its first acquisition and had bought over Quri, a US-based crowdsourcing platform. A year later, in June 2018, Boyu Capital, a prominent private equity from China, alongside GIC, Singapore's sovereign wealth fund, invested in Trax. Trax was officially on track to become the largest Singapore–Israel powerhouse. In June 2019, Hopu Investments invested in the company, bringing its valuation above US$1 billion and making Trax the second largest private technology company in Singapore and an official unicorn.

Today Trax has 9 subsidiaries, 750 employees, and 170 clients in over 50 markets. Its new Google-style offices in Singapore and Tel Aviv have been a source of envy for many, as it recruits and retains the best minds in the industry of computer vision.

Trax's vision, consistent from day one, was to digitalise the retail experience with new products and innovations every year, helping not only the retailers to reduce wastage and drive shelf efficiency and sales, but now also helping the individual shopper to find his desired products faster and with more accurate customisation to his needs. Trax is fast becoming the "Waze" of in-store navigation and the ultimate digitalised augmented offline shopping experience. Trax's vision is unfolding to become a reality and is propelling the company into new horizons.

Live with Creativity, Kindness, Determination and a Sprinkle of Luck

It is not an easy task to grow and succeed within the technology space, with overwhelmingly fast-growing competition and increasingly demanding clients. The fact that Trax enjoyed the warm and welcoming business environment in Singapore, combined with the Israeli ingenuity to innovate, adapt and pivot to customer needs using its R&D centre in Tel Aviv, were key contributors to its success.

On top of its relentless focus on product innovation and customer needs, Trax has always focused on its values-based culture and vision as a core strategy. Joel and Dror gave special attention to individual employees, and emphasised on giving back to society and helping fellow entrepreneurs.

While Dror and Joel worked tirelessly day and night, they also tried to stay balanced and enjoy time with their family and friends as much as possible. When Trax became larger and notably successful, Joel and Dror decided it would be nice to own a small leisure sailing craft to share their love of the sea with family and friends. It was only after weathering a challenging journey at sea that their boat finally arrived in Singapore. When it came to naming the boat, there was no question on what its new name should be. It was named *Mikanna,* for the friendship, hardship and exciting voyage that started thanks to two little girls — Mika and Anna.

Joel Bar-El and Dror Feldheim are founders of Trax. Joel is currently Trax's CEO, and is responsible for the company's vision, overall market strategy and execution. Dror is currently Trax's chief commercial officer, and is responsible for its global business solutions, distribution channel management, pricing and go-to-market strategy.

CPSIA information can be obtained
at www.ICGtesting.com
Printed in the USA
JSHW020845180120
3582JS00001B/19